TEACH LIKE AN MC

EDMUND ADJAPONG
LOVE.
JOY.
LIBERATION.
TEACH
LIKE
AN
MC
HIP-HOP PEDAGOGY IN THE K-12 CLASSROOM
HEINEMANN
Portsmouth, NH

Heinemann
145 Maplewood Avenue, Suite 300
Portsmouth, NH 03801
www.heinemann.com

Acknowledgments: Stebbins Ave. & Westchester Ave., Bronx © Joe Conzo Archives 2024; Elizabeth Eckford © Will Counts/The Arkansas Democrat-Gazette/AP Images; Archaelogy of Self Racial Literacy Development Model © Yolanda Sealey-Ruiz; Grandmaster Caz © Joe Conzo Archives 2024; Grafitti artist Cornbread © Johnny Nunez/WireImage/Getty Images; Wildstyle grafitti © Nikita Kapustin/Alamy; stencil grafitti © AnnetteMason/Stockimo/Alamy; bubble letter grafitti © kiyopayo/Adobe; block letter grafitti © PCJones/Alamy; *Reaching Out* © 2021 City of Philadelphia Mural Arts Program/DISTORT & Gabe Tiberino, 3221 Kensington Avenue. Photo by Steve Weinik; *Cecil B. Moore Philadelphia Freedom Fighters* © 2021 City of Philadelphia Mural Arts Program / Felix St. Fort & Gabe Tiberino, 2201 College Avenue. Photo by Steve Weinik; *We Did That* © 2021 City of Philadelphia Mural Arts Program / Letisha Bindu & Symone Salib, 13th & Arch Streets. Photo by Steve Weinik. *DEF* mural © S.E.T.H.; *Unity, Black Is Beautiful, Try II be the best version of yourself* © Robert Owusu III/iiieyeview.com; Zulu Nation patch Courtesy Smithsonian National Museum of American History.

Library of Congress Control Number: 2025930865

Printed in the United States of America on acid-free paper
ISBN-13: 978-0-325-17085-5
1 2 3 4 5 VP 29 28 27 26 25

4500906282

Editor: Louisa Irele
Production: Vicki Kasabian
Permissions: Erika Kane
Author photograph: Esston Benjamin
Cover and text designs: Suzanne Heiser
Cover and interior illustrations: Robert "THIIIRD" Owusu III
Typesetting: Kim Arney
Manufacturing: Jaime Spaulding

FOR SARA AND SAINT:

You are my greatest motivators, and
your love sustains me.

To all the **educators, community members, and parents**
who pick up this book:
Thank you for your passion and for
showing the world how hip-hop
can transform education.

To the **educators, scholars, and artists** who paved the way:
Your work and vision inspired me to take
this journey to conceptualize this book.

Finally, to **every educator** who dares
to reimagine teaching and learning:
Thank you for centering love, joy, and
liberation in your classrooms.
Your courage and commitment
make all the difference.
This book is for you and the
students you serve.

CONTENTS

FOREWORD

GLORIA LADSON-BILLINGS

I write this foreword during one of my favorite times of year . . . springtime. The grass has turned green, the trees are in bloom, and I am spending my afternoons digging in flower beds and pots as I transplant young seedlings of tomatoes, herbs, and flowers. Planting makes me think of what we as teachers do. We receive tender seedlings at various stages of growth. Some already have strong sturdy roots. Some are barely hanging on and need careful attention, good soil, watering, and fertilizing. No gardener worth their green thumbs would consider a plant *bad*! No, good gardeners look at every plant as a living thing with potential to flourish and grow. No good gardener would presume every plant needs exactly the same thing. Some of those plants will have weeds crop up around them and attempt to choke them out. Some will be inadvertently planted too close to rocky soil and will struggle to push its roots past those rocks. But, before long with careful tending and cultivation, those plants will produce a good crop.

In this volume, *Teach Like an MC: Hip-Hop Pedagogy in the K–12 Classroom*, Edmund Adjapong is using what every great teacher uses—their passion to fuel teaching and learning in their classrooms. Edmund explains how vital hip-hop was to his journey as a learner and uses it as a way to organize his teaching. The beauty of his approach is not that he is demanding everyone deploy hip-hop as a strategy for teaching and learning. For those who know hip-hop, there are at least four roles artists can assume—MC, DJ, breakdancer, and graffiti artist. Taken together an outstanding hip-hop crew produces knowledge. Edmund Adjapong argues that teachers should take on the role of MC. The hip-hop MC orchestrates the performance. They work to pull together the performance and make sure others participate and contribute in ways that best showcase their strengths. In many ways, the MC is the director and responsible for keeping things moving. The teacher who is a hip-hop MC is akin to an orchestral conductor. While they do not actually "perform" they ensure that everyone is following the score and participates in ways that help the group flow.

The teacher who teaches like an MC demonstrates why following one's passion is the key to engaged teaching and learning. Imagine a teacher whose passion is baseball. She might serve as the manager or coach. She could organize her entire classroom around helping students to improve their batting average or working toward a lower ERA. Students could follow a favorite player and use baseball trading cards to learn statistics, geography, and read and write sports columns. Or, what if a teacher has a passion for European classical music? He could serve as a conductor. He could expose students to the musical styles of composers and students can choose to follow a specific composer. They can organize their year into a symphony where each quarter is a movement. Students can learn the terminology and the aspects of symphonic performances. Perhaps students can even attend a symphony. Another teacher may have a passion for cooking. Much of what students do can be around the culinary arts. Students can start by identifying their favorite meal and the teacher can plan for students to cook that meal by year's end. Throughout the year students can learn culinary terms and equipment. Parents might participate by coming to class to do a cooking demonstration. Readers may recall a scene from the film *Stand and Deliver* featuring the work of mathematics teacher Jaime Escalante where he shows up in class with an apron, a chef's cap on his head, and a cleaver in his hand. He starts by loudly chopping an apple. Mr. Escalante used something fairly common to draw students into the mathematics class.

As a teacher educator, each week I would ask prospective teachers to come up with a metaphor for teaching. In the beginning, students came up with fairly typical responses—teacher as coach, teacher as firefighter, or teacher as parent. But as the semester wore on and students spent more time in classrooms, they began to refine their metaphors. Now I was hearing things like teacher as builder or teacher as project manager. The teacher candidates were beginning to draw from their previous work and experiences to see how teaching and its complexity could be seen as an enterprise that drew from a variety of skills and abilities. One of my favorite metaphors came from a student who seemed to struggle each week with how he would characterize teaching. He initially stuck with the more generic metaphors, but I could tell he found them unsatisfying. One day he approached me as I was walking to my car. "Professor, I think I have my metaphor!" "Well, what is it?" I asked. "Teacher as farmer! You have to till the soil, plant the seeds, do the weeding and pruning, but there are conditions and circumstances you cannot anticipate. Sometimes you get a great harvest but sometimes you may experience crop failure." I listened with interest as he excitedly detailed his understanding of teaching and his role as the teacher–farmer. I recognized that the metaphor excited him because he had a rural background. He understood farming because he grew up on a farm. Farming was one of his passions.

My own passion has always been music—all kinds of music. I grew up in a neighborhood that was home to two of the world's greatest musicians—one European Classical and the other jazz—Andre Watts and McCoy Tyner. These great musicians fueled my passion. My life is surrounded by music but early on in my teaching career I found myself attempting to conform to the norms of traditional teaching. I woke up each morning to music. I played music in the car on my drive to school. I turned on the radio in my classroom. But as soon as the bell rang, I turned off the radio! One day, because I was running late, I did not turn off the radio before the students entered the room. I rushed to turn it off and a student said, "Don't turn that off, I like that song!" I realized that I had been keeping my passion outside of the classroom. How could I expect students to enjoy and engage in a classroom to which I failed to bring my whole self? The very next day I brought in a stereo system and a stack of vinyl records. I started each class period with some music as students entered the room. During quiet times I played softer music. I started taking student requests and played the music they wanted at various portions of the class period. I introduced the students to multiple genres of music—rhythm and blues, country western, European classical, pop, Broadway show tunes, and some world or international music. While this volume focuses on teaching like an MC, I guess I could say I was teaching like a DJ!

The point of this volume is that if we are to practice culturally relevant or culturally sustaining pedagogies, we have to be authentic and show up in classrooms as whole people. Far too many of our students are trapped in classrooms with people who are "representatives" of themselves, not their true, authentic selves. These "representatives" rarely show human emotion. They are never really happy or sad or angry. They are cardboard examples of themselves, and students may fail to engage since they are unsure of the person with whom they are interacting.

Teach Like an MC is a clarion call for full and authentic engagement in the classroom. It is beseeching teachers to be fully present and involved in the lives of their students. While everyone will not necessarily appropriate the hip-hop metaphor, every teacher should work to find the passion that will allow them to connect with students in meaningful ways as previously described. *Teaching Like an MC* challenges teachers to bring energy and excitement to the classroom. This is not about trying to "entertain" students but rather to engage them in their own teaching and learning. It is about using learning theories that are tried and tested—moving students from the familiar to new learning, or what psychologists call, starting with "prior knowledge."

Teach Like an MC is wonderfully compatible with culturally relevant pedagogy. Beyond what some might see as the "fun" of being in a class with this type of teacher, the real goal is to foster students' learning, develop their cultural competence, and encourage their sociopolitical or critical consciousness. These goals should be present in every classroom and the teacher who teaches like an MC will recognize this right away.

—Gloria Ladson-Billings
Professor Emerita
University of Wisconsin–Madison

INTRODUCTION

I GOT A STORY TO TELL

Growing up, I lived on the seventeenth floor of a nineteen-story red brick apartment building in the Soundview section of the Bronx, New York. From my balcony, I had an incredible view of my community. I could see the other buildings in my apartment complex, busy streets and highways, one of the largest parks in the Bronx, and three public schools that served all the youth in my community. I also had a faint view of Manhattan's skyline and communities outside the Bronx that felt distant and excluded those who looked like me. People who were outsiders to my neighborhood would insist I lived in public housing or the projects because I lived in an apartment building in the Bronx. During my childhood, I did not have many experiences or interactions with people who were racially different from me. As a child, being Black was all I knew. The Soundview section of the Bronx at the time was predominantly Black. Most of my peers in my elementary school identified as Black. At home, whenever my parents had visitors, all the older women were to be called "auntie" out of respect, even if I didn't know them at all. At school, I greeted my friends with elaborate and multistep handshakes; my friends and I all had similar interests. We all had an appreciation and love for hip-hop. We would compete to see who could recite hip-hop songs such as "Ms. Jackson" by Outkast. We wore white T-shirts and all-white Air Force Ones as if it was our uniform. Our styles were inspired by hip-hop culture—Black culture. Even as a child, being Black was rich and multifaceted and always meant holding myself up with high regard. It was with time and my experiences in schools that I gained insight into how people's perceptions of the identities that I found so much pride and joy in owning could negatively impact my experiences in school.

While my elementary school was located within my community, where I felt comfortable and safe, I would go to school fearful of the adults in the school building who were assumed to protect and help create a comfortable learning environment for me. Most of my teachers were outsiders to my community who traveled into my neighborhood to teach those they viewed as worthy of their instruction and to terrorize others. Nearly all of the teachers in my elementary school were White women. Every day I feared that my teachers would find an action, a comment, or even a question of mine to be inappropriate and, in response, reprimand me. I was fearful of my teachers, who did not understand me or my reality as a Black boy and viewed all of my actions as problematic. I did not sense that my teachers were there to demonstrate their love for me, nor did they see my questions or perspectives as sparked by curiosity or centered in a drive to learn and be challenged.

I remember constantly getting into trouble and being reprimanded for a number of reasons that did not make sense to me. In third grade, my teacher was escorting my class from the cafeteria to our classroom upstairs as usual. We were walking on the right side of the hallway in silence with our right index finger covering our lips in two perfectly straight lines in size order, one for boys and one for girls. Following our teacher, the class walked down the hallway near the principal's office. Our teacher told us to stop. The entire class halted. As my class practiced the life skill of standing still, I felt a tickle on my head and began to scratch it. My teacher noticed a movement toward the back of the boy's line. She verbally reprimanded me in front of my peers and walked me into the main office to call my father to explain that I had a hard time following directions. I remember thinking to myself, *If the teacher had to scratch her head, she would, so why would I be getting in trouble for doing the same? Where else in the world do I ever walk anywhere in silence with my fingers to my lips?* The rules felt restraining and meant to teach us to be the same. The lessons, both social and academic, seemed to be focused on order and meant to teach us about self-control, as opposed to being centered on encouraging us to be free thinkers or providing opportunities to think critically or to question. But I knew that even thinking about this, let alone sharing it with anyone, would only give adults more reason to think I was trying to be a troublemaker.

My parents were heavily involved in my education to my teachers' benefit. They attended every parent–teacher conference and tried their best to help me with my homework at night, even though neither of them graduated from high school. They were very responsive to teachers, so whenever I did something that a teacher deemed inappropriate or unacceptable, the teacher would either threaten to call my parents or actually follow through with that threat. In Ghana, where my parents were raised, teachers are highly respected. They are viewed as professionals who are passionate about imparting knowledge unto students and genuinely encouraging the holistic development of all students intellectually, physically, morally, and ethically. My parents never questioned whether my teachers truly had my best interest at heart. But from a young age, I had always felt that my teachers could not and/or did not care to see me or know me outside of what they had determined to be true about my identities. When I arrived home, as expected, my father was upset with me and asked me why I had a difficult time following the teacher's directions, and I found myself with no reasonable explanation.

Despite my *rebellious* behavior, in the fifth grade, my teachers identified me as a student whom they believed to be gifted and talented because of my performance on standardized state tests. I was recommended to attend a gifted and talented middle school in the district. The middle school was about three miles away from my neighborhood, and was vastly different than what I had ever experienced. To get to school, I rode on a public-school bus for forty-five minutes, as opposed to walking down the street from my apartment. When I got off the bus, I had to walk through streets lined with beautiful brick houses that sat behind large maplewood trees to get to my new school. There were no tall apartment buildings, nor were the streets busy with adults rushing to work and children rushing to school, like my neighborhood. The streets were quiet, so quiet that you could hear the leaves scratching the concrete on a crisp fall day. When I first arrived at middle school, I realized that not only was the neighborhood different from what I was accustomed to, but the demographics of students were also different from anything that I'd experienced. Most of the students who attended my middle school were White and from the school's surrounding community.

As a sixth grader, I did not fully understand why my parents wanted me to attend the gifted school, besides it being perceived as a "good school." Even though the school was supposed to be better than other public schools, I didn't see much of a difference. The school aides still wouldn't let me express my joy in replicating hip-hop beats on the cafeteria tables with my hands. During recess, games like tag were prohibited. The teachers sat us in rows and limited student interaction. We were expected to soak in content as our teachers talked *to* us, class after class. In one of my math classes, I was encouraged to learn algebra using a computer program, with no guidance from the teacher in the room. In other classes, I just copied notes into my notebook and was expected to demonstrate my understanding of those notes on an assessment. In my discontent, I continued to wonder what about this school was better than the one in my own neighborhood. The only difference I could determine was that I had to travel to and from school, and I felt isolated from my friends from my neighborhood.

My science class was the only part of the day that I looked forward to because I had an opportunity to learn about natural phenomena. Since my participation in a life cycle lab in my elementary school, I had a passion for science that emerged after liberating butterflies we had been observing metaphorize.

Toward the end of my sixth-grade year, I decided to participate in the annual science fair as a way of engaging with my new school community. I chose to study the effect that orange juice had on the growth of a plant. I remember watering a plant with orange juice and putting it in my closet, where I would observe its growth for weeks. My mom was frustrated with me because of the odor that permeated from the plant through the closet door.

The day before the science fair, I stayed up all night working tirelessly on my trifold board, printing and gluing pieces of paper onto the board until I was completely satisfied and proud of the product. I traveled on the crowded bus to school with the large, bulky, and difficult-to-carry trifold board. I got to school, eager to show my science teacher my science fair project so she could acknowledge my hard work and brilliance. She reviewed my procedure and conclusion. She shook her head and explained that I could not present my project at the science fair because it was incomplete. Shortly and simply, she explained that I failed to include a control group in my experiment and therefore had no group to compare my experimental group with. I was devastated, and for the remainder of my middle school years, I found myself disengaged in school due to that "failed experience" in science. At that very moment, I started to doubt my academic ability and started to believe that if I could not be successful in science, a subject I loved, then how could I be successful in any other subject matter? This lack of empathy and guidance further alienated me from school.

My teachers rarely called on me, provided feedback that would support my understanding of content, or helped me outside of the classroom to catch up on my work. In the school for the gifted and talented, the perception teachers had of me as the problem child and the child who did not want to learn persisted. I sensed that the teachers at my middle school did not understand or try to understand my experiences and, therefore, could not relate to me in terms of delivering content and building positive relationships. As a result of disengagement from school, I developed the persona of the class clown to keep my attention throughout the school day. I made jokes about anyone or anything to make the day entertaining for myself. I found joy in distracting my peers. I found joy in making teachers upset. Ultimately, I wanted to know how well the teacher would react to my distractions. My parents were called to the school many times to meet with the guidance counselor to develop behavior intervention plans and discuss incentives to get me to produce better quality work or perform better on state assessments. Although I developed an identity and reputation as the class clown, I felt *stupid* and isolated in the school for gifted and talented students. As a result, I spent most of my time in middle school guarded and closed off to learning. There was no space in my school for me to be my authentic self, nor did I see myself in the content the way I had seen myself in the butterflies. As a result, I was not successful academically.

By the time I arrived at high school, I was only going to school because, in my household, not going to school was not an option. I went to a high school with a focused curriculum catered to nursing and health professions in the Bronx. On the first day of high school, I walked into my ninth-grade physics class and was introduced to my first Black male educator. Not only was the ninth-grade physics teacher a Black male, but he was from the Bronx. He talked like us, understood us, and used hip-hop to teach us. Not only would we listen to hip-hop songs in class, but we learned science through analogies and references to hip-hop artifacts. We examined rapper 50 Cent's G-Unit chain as a pendulum to support our understanding of motion, gravity, inertia, and centripetal force. I understood hip-hop and using it as a conduit for instruction spoke to my joy. I took the time to love myself as a student and the identities I brought to the classroom because he taught with humanity and acknowledged our culture while also holding me to high standards of learning. The difference in his teaching practice was his ability to provide access to the content through his willingness to learn about me and my peers. This was my teacher's way of demonstrating that because he understood our joy, he could teach us with love. My interest and engagement in school was sparked in that physics class because my teacher understood the power and potential of using hip-hop to engage his students. Finally, after navigating schools for more than nine years, I felt comfortable in a classroom because I saw myself reflected in the content. My passion for science was reignited. This unique and unexpected experience in a science classroom so many years after the metamorphosis lab allowed me to sustain my interests in the sciences during high school and motivated me to further explore these interests in college.

Fascinated by the common references in hip-hop culture and music and eager to study biochemistry, I enrolled in a college program with the goal of becoming a pharmacist. Though I was inspired by hip-hop culture and fueled with the reignition of my passion for science, when

I arrived at a state college in rural upstate New York, I had a hard time sleeping because it was too quiet at night. The quiet lull of the city's trains, buses, and cars was no longer there to comfort me. This rural environment, though unfamiliar and new, resurfaced remnants of previous educational experiences from middle school. In this new but familiar setting, I sat silently and isolated in the sea of rowed seats as I watched my peers access their prior knowledge to answer questions in my introduction to biology and chemistry classes that I was not remotely familiar with. Now older and more perceptive of the educational experiences I had, this higher education experience forced me to reflect and question my K–12 school experiences deeply. What was it exactly about my experiences that had put me so far behind my peers in basic science content knowledge?

Though I ultimately persisted in the biochemistry program, I continued to struggle. Many of the students of color from New York City who also struggled did not persist. They changed their majors from the sciences to other programs within the college. I continued to question why this phenomenon disproportionately impacted students of color. This realization that students who looked and talked like me were dropping the program motivated me to work twice as hard as my peers to reach the level of understanding necessary to succeed in the biochemistry program. But I continued to question why that hustle was even necessary to begin with. Ultimately, I reached an epiphany that my teachers in urban schools simply did not know how to teach me or my multiple cultures and identities. Growing up, it was clear that my teachers, whether teaching in a school within my community or not, did not understand my culture, my identity, or my experiences as a young Black boy, and there weren't many attempts on their part to learn. I had experienced that when science was the most relevant, it was joyful and liberatory, and when my teacher expressed high standards along with support, it demonstrated love and care for me as a whole student.

My college professors did not provide joy, liberation, or love in their pedagogy. Their greatest concern was centered on exams and regurgitating information, as my middle school had so heavily focused on. Still, fueled by the reignition of my passion for science from my high school experience and my drive to prove everyone wrong, I persisted as the only person of color who graduated with a degree in biochemistry and biology in a class of about fifty students who majored in the sciences.

While my personal educational experiences are unique to me, they are not the only source of inspiration for my work on bridging connections between hip-hop and education. My experiences as a student in public schools were at times, daunting, traumatic, and unexplainable. I never felt comfortable or fully self-actualized in any of my schooling experiences (Maslow 1965). With little knowledge of who I truly was, it was difficult for my teachers to teach content in engaging ways that I found relevant and interesting. When I reflect on my K–12 school experience, I recall feeling like my teachers did not truly understand who I was or any of the various identities that I brought into the school building as a Black boy from an urban community and immigrant family who participated consciously and unconsciously in hip-hop culture. As a result of my negative experiences as a student, I decided to become a teacher to support youth from the Bronx, and similar communities to make meaningful connections to learning. However, as a first-year middle school science educator in the Bronx, I found myself standing in front of students with whom I shared a racial and communal identity with, but who I struggled to reach academically. I found myself using teacher identities, voices, and practices that were not my own. These teacher identities and practices came naturally to me because it is what I knew. I was planning and teaching solely from a dated textbook that was given to me, lecturing sixth-grade students and expecting them to retain content information. I was frustrated with students who did not connect with my approach to teaching.

Noticing that my students we disengaged and not performing well on assessments made me reflect and reconsider my approach to teaching. I realized that although I shared a common Black identity with my students, we were still very different—we were a part of different generations and as a result had different life experiences. This realization prompted me to explore my students' interests. All I had to do was ask and listen. Luckily, students are perceptive, genuine, and honest and they will tell you about yourself whether you are ready to hear it or not. I showed interest in my students' interests in ways I wished my teachers had done for me. I created space for my students to explore their own identities and their relationship to science as we learned science content which brought me back to hip-hop's way of teaching. In listening to the voices in my classroom, I was able to find my own. My eagerness to reject tired traditional teaching practices and my aspiration to grow and learn from my students fueled by the memories of my own negative educational experiences showed me the connection between myself, my students, and the transformative nature of hip-hop culture and its potential in providing joy, love, and liberation for students. Drawing from the frameworks of culturally relevant, responsive, and sustaining pedagogies, I identified my teaching practice as hip-hop pedagogy (Adjapong 2017). The more I made space for students to share, the more I learned about their needs and interests. I quickly realized that my students, regardless of their background, had some connection to hip-hop culture whether consciously or subconsciously, and students engaged in hip-hop through music, art, dance, and their use of technology. Through this new lens of seeing my students, I also noticed how hip-hop identities existed outside of the classroom. Hip-hop's captivating allure and pull was in the hallways, at lunch, and even in the principal's office. This encouraged me to explore the explicit connection between hip-hop culture and teaching to support other educators in creating engaging, culturally responsive, and critical learning moments while leveraging hip-hop as youth culture.

While interrogating hip-hop's influence and potential power for transforming educational experiences in schools, I reached an understanding of how common these experiences pertaining to the intersections of race, community, and schooling are for Black and Brown youth. Surviving the perception of being a "child with a problem" inspired me to find answers and solutions to these educational disparities across New York City. Unfortunately, my educational experience is not unique to me. In fact, many Black and Brown youth have negative experiences as it relates to education. Thus, it became even more important for me to create a teaching framework informed by hip-hop culture that would support educators who had also become teachers to stop the cycle of poor teaching and to nurture positive educational experiences for all youth, with special attention to youth with culturally diverse backgrounds who also deserve positive and affirming educational experiences. My story serves as a poignant reminder of the profound impact that community, race, and education have on students' lives. My story emphasizes the need for educational systems that are not only inclusive and understanding of students' diverse backgrounds but also are capable of nurturing and celebrating the unique identities of every student.

Hip-hop, in many ways, serves as a testament to the undying spirit and innovative brilliance of Black communities and their ongoing fight toward Black liberation.

HIP-HOP
101

Understanding Hip-Hop Culture and Pedagogy

Most students in schools today feel a need for transformative pedagogies. For decades, education policymakers and stakeholders have worked toward crafting policies that will improve the rates of achievement in public schools across the nation. Unfortunately, many of the nation's attempts to reform education have fallen short of the intended outcomes. The most recent education reform policies, No Child Left Behind (NCLB) and Every Student Succeeds Act (ESSA), have received harsh criticism from educators and have had the most direct impact on how our classrooms operate today.

From 2002 to 2015, NCLB held schools and, in particular, teachers accountable for the achievement of students and heavily emphasized standardized assessments that masked the truth behind why schools were failing: lack of engaging and relevant curriculum and pedagogy (Gay 2007; Guisbond 2012). The Every Student Succeeds

Act (ESSA), implemented in 2015 as a response to counter the negative implications of NCLB, required states to adopt new and "challenging" academic standards in reading, math, and science, also known as the Common Core State Standards (CCSS). While the CCSS was initially viewed as an opportunity for schools to innovate and move away from a top-down, one-size-fits-all solution to low academic performance, it also came with a new set of high-stakes Common Core testing for students.

Scholars argue that the hyper-emphasis on standardized testing over the last few decades has shifted the focus away from effective classroom pedagogy that engages students and makes them curious about the content (Au 2007; Hamilton et al. 2007). Teachers now focus most of their instruction on preparing students for standardized exams, which often includes test-prep lessons where students find themselves practicing test questions out of booklets, as opposed to learning content through culturally relevant approaches to instruction and curricula that connects new understandings to students' lived experiences. In addition to an overemphasis on high-stakes testing, schools nationwide face a number of challenges that have been cited to negatively impact student achievement, including limited resources (Baker and Di Carlo 2020), teacher shortages (Anderson 2023), lack of racial diversity among teachers (Rucinski 2023), lack of culturally relevant pedagogical knowledge (Underwood and Mensah 2018), and inequitable school discipline policies (Carter Andrews, and Gutwein 2020), to name a few. Schools across the nation are struggling to find ways to create learning experiences that are truly catered to the needs and interests of students.

As my own story shows, these challenges, however, aren't new. Historically, schools have not been an inviting space for students, as they don't reflect students' cultures and are absent of student's voices. Consequently, lack of student voice and culture leads to a decrease interest in learning. Therefore, there is a need to provide school communities with effective teaching and learning frameworks that extend beyond testing culture.

UNDERSTANDING ASSET-BASED AND CULTURALLY COMPETENT PEDAGOGIES

Studies have shown that educators often underestimate the academic potential of students of color (Cherng 2017; Ferguson 2003; McKown and Weinstein 2008). These educators typically set lower expectations for students of color and view their cultural differences as obstacles and barriers rather than as beneficial to learning. In response to this deficit view of students of color, educational experts have devised various teaching methods collectively known as asset-based pedagogies. Asset-based pedagogies are approaches to teaching that embrace and integrate the cultural identities and personal experiences of students as key elements of effective teaching. Well-known examples of asset-based pedagogies are culturally relevant pedagogy, culturally responsive teaching, and culturally sustaining pedagogy. These approaches to teaching share a common theme as they prioritize the knowledge and perspectives of communities that have historically been marginalized in educational settings (Figure 1–1).

Asset-Based and Culturally Competent Pedagogies	Definition	Seminal Text
Culturally Relevant Pedagogy	Pedagogical practices that help students become academically successful, cultivate cultural competence, and develop critical consciousness.	Ladson-Billings, G. 1995. "Toward a Theory of Culturally Relevant Pedagogy." *American Educational Research Journal* 32 (3): 465–491.

Continues

Continued from previous page

Asset-Based and Culturally Competent Pedagogies	Definition	Seminal Text
Culturally Responsive Pedagogy	Culturally responsive teaching is defined as using the cultural characteristics, experiences, and perspectives of ethnically diverse students as conduits for teaching them more effectively. It assumes that when academic knowledge and skills are situated within the lived experiences and frames of reference of students, they are more personally meaningful, have higher interest appeal, and are learned more quickly and thoroughly (Gay 2002).	Gay, G. 2002. "Preparing for Culturally Responsive Teaching." *Journal of Teacher Education* 53 (2): 106–116.
Culturally Sustaining Pedagogy	Culturally sustaining pedagogy (CSP) is a critical framework for centering and sustaining Indigenous, Black, Latinx, Asian, and Pacific Islander communities as these memberships necessarily intersect with gender and sexuality, dis/ability, class, language, land, and more.	Alim, H. S., D. Paris, and C. P. Wong. 2020. "Culturally Sustaining Pedagogies: A Critical Framework for Centering Communities." In *Handbook of the Cultural Foundations of Learning*, edited by N. S. Nasir, C. D. Lee, R. Pea, and M. Mckinney de Royston, 261–276. New York: Routledge.
Hip-Hop Pedagogy	Hip-hop pedagogy is an approach to teaching that encourages educators to gain authentic understandings of their students' cultures and develop their own personal critical consciousness and that of their students while incorporating hip-hop's creative elements and sensibilities in teaching practices and curricula choices.	

Figure 1–1 • A Breakdown of Asset-Based Culturally Competent Pedagogies

What Does It Mean to Be Culturally Responsive?

Many educators and scholars use the terms *culturally responsive, culturally relevant, and culturally sustaining* interchangeably to communicate a range of ideas that highlight the value of respecting and honoring students' cultures across educational contexts. The three theories of practice have similar aims to support the academic achievement of students of diverse cultural, ethnic, linguistic, and racial backgrounds through teaching practices that affirm the various components that make up students' identities. Elements of all three pedagogies can be found in hip-hop pedagogy (Figure 1–2).

Culturally Relevant Pedagogy

Culturally Relevant Pedagogy was conceptualized by Gloria Ladson-Billings through her extensive research in schools with Black educators, where she sought to redefine narratives around Black student achievement as well as counteract deficit views of Black youth. Culturally Relevant Pedagogy is defined as a "theoretical model

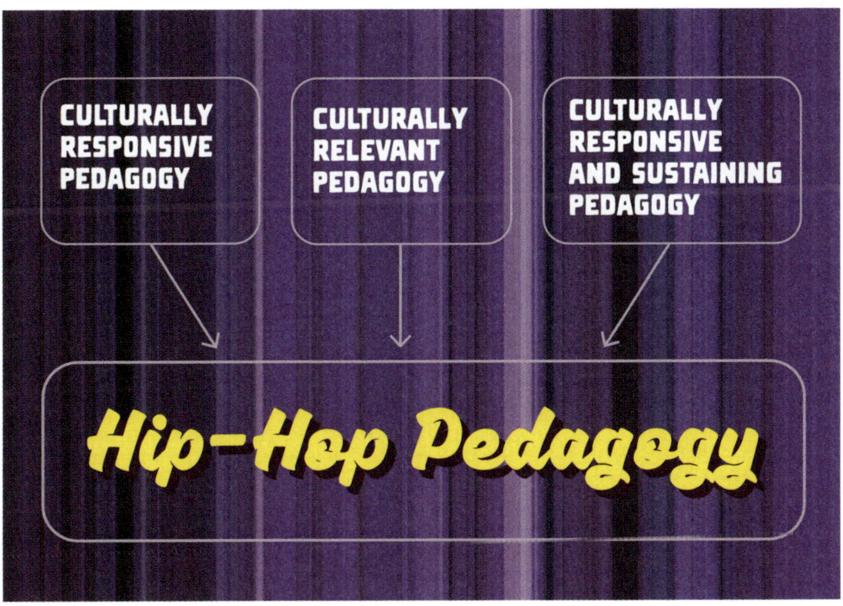

Figure 1–2 • Asset-based pedagogies that inform hip-hop pedagogy

that not only addresses student achievement but also helps students to accept and affirm their cultural identity while developing critical perspectives that challenge inequities that schools (and other institutions) perpetuate" (Ladson-Billings 1995, 469). A teacher employing culturally relevant pedagogy operates under the belief that students from every racial, ethnic, and cultural background are capable of academic success. This approach to teaching recognizes that students can exhibit their cultural competence in a variety of ways, which should be privileged in the classroom. Further, a culturally relevant teacher is aware and encourages students to be aware and critical of both societal and educational systems that perpetuate injustices (Ladson-Billings 1995). Ladson-Billings stresses the significance of the teacher–student relationship and the importance of teachers understanding and acknowledging that the diverse identities of their students significantly influence their educational experience. Therefore, culturally relevant teaching is a way to "empower students intellectually, socially, emotionally, and politically by using cultural referents to impart knowledge, skills, and attitudes" (1994, 18).

Culturally Responsive Pedagogy

Culturally Responsive Pedagogy was conceptualized by Geneva Gay (2018) as she advocated for a "paradigmatic shift in the pedagogy used with non-middle-class, non–European American students in U.S. schools" (25). Culturally responsive teaching is defined as "using the cultural knowledge, prior experiences, frames of reference, and performance styles of ethnically diverse students to make learning encounters more relevant to and effective for them" (36). Gay highlights that culturally responsive teaching "filters curriculum, content, and teaching strategies through their cultural frames of reference to make the content more personally meaningful and easier to master," which traditional instructional ideologies fail to do for students of diverse backgrounds (32). Further, Gay argues that culturally responsive pedagogy is inherently "radical because it makes explicit the previously implicit role of culture in teaching and learning, and it insists that educational institutions accept the legitimacy and viability of ethnic-group cultures in improving learning outcomes" (32). Ultimately, it argues that culture is essential to effective instruction, and educational institutions must acknowledge and privilege students' cultures to support and improve student learning outcomes.

Culturally Sustaining Pedagogy

Culturally Sustaining Pedagogy was conceptualized by Django Paris and Samy Alim and "is a critical educational framework that seeks to recognize, sustain, and center the cultural practices, identities, and knowledge of diverse communities, particularly those historically marginalized by systemic inequalities" (Alim, Paris, and Wong 2020, 261). This framework serves as an extension of previously discussed asset-based pedagogies, such as culturally relevant pedagogy, to explicitly articulate and advocate for the sustenance of systemically marginalized communities and students' diverse identities within the school community. Culturally Sustaining Pedagogy is an approach to instruction that recognizes that culture is a dynamic set of values, beliefs, and practices that varies across students' social identities (including, but not limited to, race, gender, sexuality, disability, socioeconomic status, and geographical location) and should be sustained by school communities. "Culturally Sustaining Pedagogy advocates for an educational approach that not only acknowledges centuries of oppression and domination but also draws on the resilience, resistance, and revolutionary spirit of marginalized communities. This pedagogy emphasizes the importance of sustaining and revitalizing cultural [and linguistic] practices and beliefs as acts of resistance against racialized white terror and oppression" (262). The aim of Culturally Sustaining Pedagogy is to "transform education into a space that sustains and nurtures the lifeways and potentials of all communities, particularly those that have been historically marginalized and oppressed" (262).

Overall, Culturally Relevant, Responsive, and Sustaining Pedagogies each present a nuanced approach to education, emphasizing the importance of acknowledging and integrating students' diverse cultural backgrounds into the learning environment and instruction.

While Culturally Relevant Pedagogy focuses on affirming students' cultural identities, academic rigor of student curricula, and challenging institutional inequities, Culturally Responsive Pedagogy centers on adapting teaching methods to match the cultural contexts of diverse students, thereby enhancing their learning experience. Finally, Culturally Sustaining Pedagogy extends these concepts by actively sustaining and revitalizing the cultural practices of historically marginalized communities. Collectively, asset-based pedagogies emphasize a shift in traditional educational paradigms, moving away from a one-size-fits-all approach to one that is deeply rooted in cultural empathy, responsiveness, sustainability, and liberatory practices. They highlight the necessity of creating educational spaces that are not only inclusive but also liberatory, where both educators and students critique society through their expanded understandings of political, social, and historical knowledge while fostering an environment where all students can thrive both academically and personally.

ARE YOU A CULTURALLY COMPETENT EDUCATOR?

Directions: On the following page are competencies of a culturally competent educator. Self-assess with your own practices in mind and return to these competencies periodically to see which areas you hope to develop further.

- Which of these competencies do you need to develop?
- What steps will you take as an educator to become increasingly culturally competent?
- Set an intention around an identified competency you'd like to focus and improve on while engaging with this book.

Indicators of a Culturally Competent Educator

INDICATOR	DESCRIPTION
Cultural Competence and Awareness	Understand students' various cultural backgrounds and how these influence students' learning experiences and identities.
Cultural Sustenance and Advocacy	Actively work to sustain and celebrate the cultural practices and identities of all students, especially those from historically marginalized communities.
Student-Centered Approach	Prioritize the unique needs and backgrounds of each student, fostering an environment where diverse perspectives and learning styles are valued.
Inclusive Curriculum Design	Develop and implement a curriculum that reflects the diversity of cultures and experiences of students.
Resilience and Resistance Emphasis	Incorporate and highlight the stories of resilience and resistance from marginalized communities into curricula.
Empowerment and Advocacy Skills	Empower students to affirm their cultural identities and advocate for themselves in challenging systemic inequities within and outside the classroom.

Continues

Continued from previous page

INDICATOR	DESCRIPTION
Adaptability in Teaching Methods	Adapt teaching styles to align with the cultural contexts and learning styles of diverse students.
Collaborate with Families and Local Community	Collaborate with families and local community members to situate learning in the context of the local community. See yourself as a member of the community.

The competencies in this chart describe qualities of an educator who is ready to dive into hip-hop pedagogy work. To successfully engage in hip-hop pedagogy, you must know yourself well. You must be aware of your areas of strength and your areas that need improvement.

WHAT IS HIP-HOP PEDAGOGY?

Hip-hop pedagogy is informed by and builds upon the frameworks of culturally relevant, responsive, and sustaining pedagogies. From culturally relevant pedagogy, hip-hop pedagogy encourages educators to develop their personal critical consciousness as well as their students' critical consciousness. From culturally responsive pedagogy, hip-hop pedagogy encourages educators to see and value hip-hop culture as a youth culture that students participate in and one that empowers young people globally. From culturally sustaining pedagogy, hip-hop pedagogy encourages educators and school communities to leverage the essential elements of hip-hop culture as teaching approaches to create curricula that encourage students to engage and utilize hip-hop culture and sensibilities to make sense of content and the world around them.

Hip-hop pedagogy encourages you to gain an authentic understanding of hip-hop culture, and as a result, supports you in developing the critical consciousness necessary to understand how your students participate and engage in their identified cultures. Educators, thus, become more understanding and aware of other marginalized groups, empowering educators to leverage student cultures in an authentic and engaging manner. I define hip-hop pedagogy as a teaching approach that motivates educators to authentically understand their students' cultural backgrounds and cultivate both their own and their students' critical consciousness. This method integrates the creative elements (knowledge of self, MC, graffiti, DJ, and breakdancing) and sensibilities of hip-hop into educational practices and curriculum decisions. Throughout this text, you will uncover the history of each creative element and its connection to teaching and learning. Hip-hop pedagogy encourages educators and school communities to privilege hip-hop culture and sensibilities within academic spaces to sustain students' connection to Black culture and utilize ways of engagement that are informed by hip-hop culture. Hip-hop pedagogy is not only for Black and students from diverse backgrounds. Hip-hop pedagogy is not only about the incorporation of hip-hop music in the classroom. The goal of utilizing hip-hop pedagogy is to invite students to develop a connection with content while leveraging their culture, realities, and experiences to reach them on their cultural turf.

What can hip-hop teach school communities about youth empowerment and learning? How is hip-hop culture different from hip-hop music? To start, hip-hop pedagogy is anchored in the five creative elements of hip-hop, which include MC, graffiti art, breakdancing, DJ, and knowledge of self, and thus is a grander phenomenon than its musical output. Young people who consume and identify as part of hip-hop culture engage in hip-hop's creative elements in their everyday lives. Thus, hip-hop pedagogy acts as a vehicle to incorporate youth culture into the daily instruction of all content areas with the goal of creating opportunities for all students to creatively engage and access content.

Is it hip-hop or hip hop?

Within hip-hop culture, the spelling and presentation of the term "hip-hop" have often varied, influenced by the culture's informal and creative nature. Early pioneers, artists, and writers in hip-hop culture often played with language, spelling, and typography, which led to variations in how "hip-hop or hip hop" has been written over the years. However, the presence of the hyphen has been relatively consistent in foundational hip-hop texts and popular cultural artifacts. While the non-hyphenated form has become more relevant in academic spaces, as some argue, "hip-hop" refers to commercialized and product-based representations of the culture. I argue that using the hyphen is seen as a way to honor hip-hop's origins and its interconnected elements, highlighting the unity between its artistic forms and cultural significance. Debating the presentation of the term "hip-hop" can overshadow the deeper and more meaningful work of interrogating and uplifting the culture through research, education, and artistic expression. Language evolves organically within communities, and trying to impose rigid standards on a term like "hip-hop," which is rooted in fluidity and creativity, can risk missing the essence of what the culture stands for.

Hip-Hop as Love

Hip-hop culture has been deeply intertwined with Black culture since its inception. It is an exemplar of the Black experience in America and has always highlighted the love and admiration that Black people have for their communities and culture. Hip-hop promotes love as a universal force that can unite people of all backgrounds and cultures. From its roots in the Bronx in the 1970s to its global influence today, hip-hop continues to serve as a powerful tool for expressing the struggles, triumphs, and multiplicities of Black communities around the world. Hip-hop has provided a platform for Black voices to be heard and has brought attention to important issues facing Black communities in mainstream America. Hip-hop artists have used their music to uplift their communities, inspire change, and celebrate their culture. Thus, hip-hop has been a powerful tool for expressing love for Black communities and promoting unity and pride among Black people.

Hip-hop educators exemplify love in their classrooms by having high expectations for students at all times. Teachers form expectations of their students' achievements based on the knowledge they have of students, including (1) how students perform in class, (2) their previous grades, and (3) teachers' prejudices and/or stereotypes (implicit and explicit). The expectations that teachers have of their students have been shown to impact students' future achievement—this effect is recognized as the Pygmalion effect (Figure 1–3). The Pygmalion effect refers to "the effects of interpersonal expectancies, that is, the finding that what one person expects of another can come to serve as a self-fulfilling prophecy" (Rosenthal 2010, 1398). In other words, a teacher's high expectations can lead to higher academic performance of their students, and a teacher's low expectations can lead to low academic

Figure 1–3 • The Pygmalion effect can create a self-fulfilling prophesy.

performance of their students. Our beliefs about our students' abilities influence our actions toward students, which in turn impacts other's beliefs about themselves. A hip-hop pedagogy educator can understand and appreciate students' cultures and complex identities as assets for teaching and learning. Once we are genuinely able to appreciate who our students are and how they show up in our classrooms without wanting to change them, we are able to fully accept them without minimizing our expectations of what they are able to achieve. Rather, through love, educators can use their understanding of students to support them in gaining the skills, competencies, and knowledge that support students in becoming who and what they want to be.

Hip-Hop as Joy

Hip-hop, with its upbeat rhythms and lively beats, has always been synonymous with joy. Since its beginning, hip-hop culture provides opportunities and space where participants can be their authentic selves, experience belonging, and validation around shared experiences of marginalization. This space of joy, although not always protected, distinguishes authentic participants (those who engage by receiving the call of action against injustice) from those who are inauthentic (those who simply engage in hip-hop's joy). It must be made clear that although hip-hop preferences authenticity and the shared experience of marginalized people, due to its inclusive nature, it doesn't exclude those who have not yet gained authenticity for themselves or who do not come from a historically marginalized group. This is the power of the joy of hip-hop because it invites those who may be outsiders to join the group. Thus, what can make you inauthentic or authentic to hip-hop is what you choose to do with the joy that hip-hop offers its participants. I argue that participants who do not (and even those who do) identify as part of historically marginalized groups should use their privilege and access to critique, interrogate, and address injustice experienced by participants of the hip-hop community.

Hip-hop is that safe space where joy can be actualized for many youth and adults in a society that holds negative perceptions of historically marginalized groups. In her book *Unearthing Joy*, Gholdy Muhammad (2023) explains that "joy is also related to advancing happiness by elevating beauty in humanity, as well as embracing truthful narratives and representations of diverse people of the world (including our students)." Hip-hop culture offers a space where historically marginalized groups see their lives and cultures represented in authentic and relatable ways. Through its music, dance, art, and fashion, hip-hop celebrates diverse backgrounds and experiences while fostering a sense of pride in identity. In our schools and classrooms, educators can leverage hip-hop as an approach to create opportunities and spaces for joy to be actualized. When hip-hop is effectively utilized across educational spaces, we can encourage young people to be their authentic selves, celebrate the diversity of students' cultures and identities, and draw connections between content, curricula, and students while interrogating and countering inequities that contribute to the oppression of groups. This calls for a teacher's ability to adapt to teaching methods that may require them to know the difference between hip-hop culture in the Bronx vs. hip-hop culture in Atlanta, acknowledging their differences and leveraging what's most appropriate for student groups (Figure 1–4).

Similarly, hip-hop music offers artists the opportunity to share their stories and realities as counter-storytelling. Through counter-storytelling, artists communicate their experiences and reveal the often distorted or overlooked realities of historically oppressed groups. Hip-hop provides a platform for these communities to voice their authentic experiences, struggles, and aspirations. Many artists challenge social norms and address injustice in their music, offering narratives of resistance, empowerment, and calls to action. As a result, hip-hop serves as a contested space to be your authentic self, experience community, and advocate for social change, while enhancing a collective sense of purpose and a sense of empowerment. Leveraging hip-hop and youth culture across educational spaces, specifically through pedagogy and classroom instruction, can aid in creating school systems that truly reflect and honor the cultures and identities of students while fostering joy for learning through youth culture.

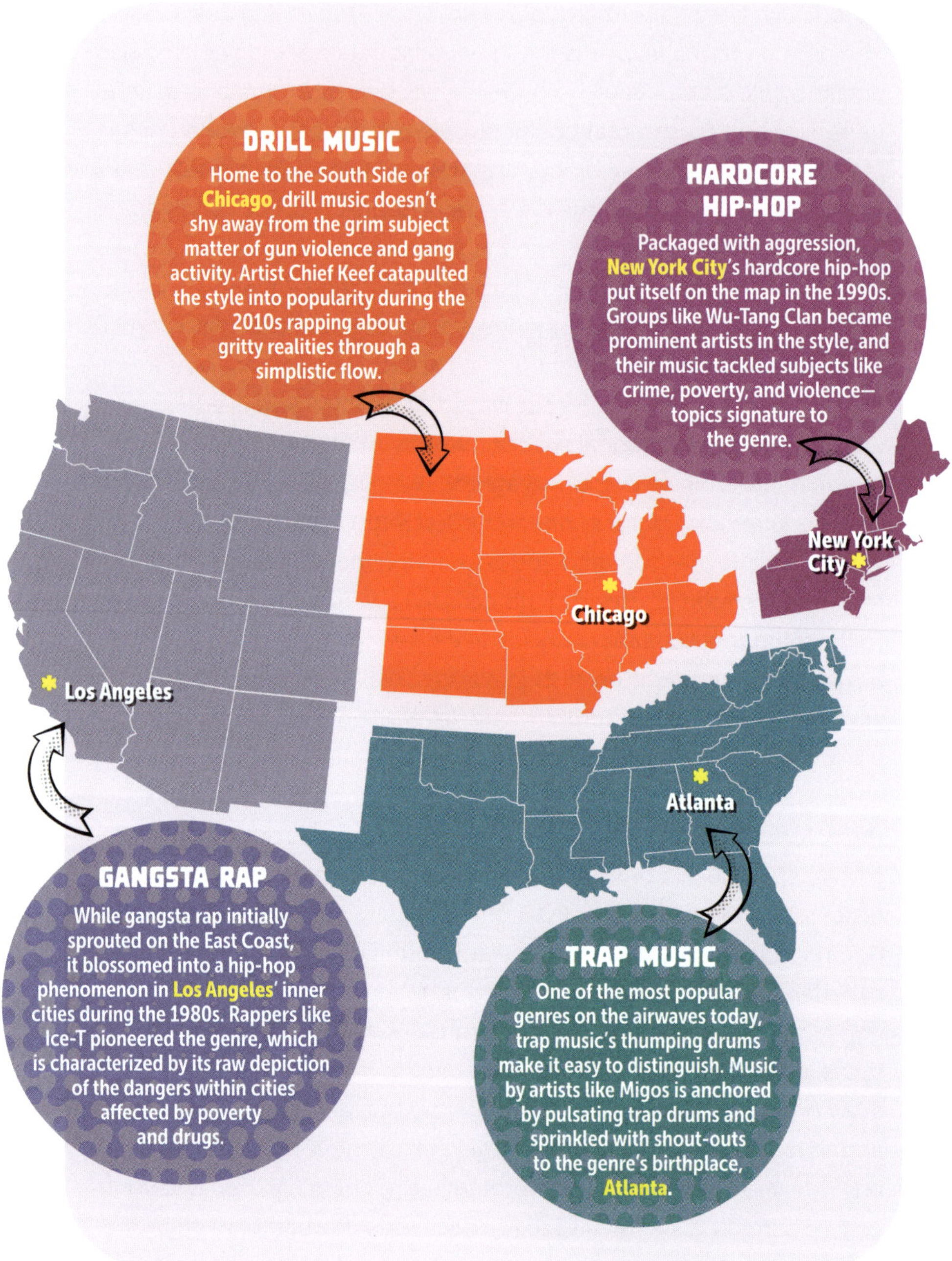

Figure 1–4 • Subgenres of hip-hop music and the geographic location that shaped them

Hip-Hop as Liberation

In addition to exemplifying joy, hip-hop has always been a powerful tool for liberation, giving voice to communities that have experienced systemic marginalization. Hip-hop offers a platform for individuals to express their realities and challenges and to interrogate and address social injustice. Through its creative elements, hip-hop has empowered countless people from all backgrounds to speak out against racism, poverty, police brutality, mass incarceration, and other forms of oppression. Hip-hop has played a pivotal role in the struggle for liberation and social justice for Black communities, in particular by inspiring individuals to take action and effect positive change. Hip-hop has served as the backdrop for all social movements where Black communities have advocated for justice and equality. For example, during the global Black Lives Matter protests of 2020 sparked by the deaths of Breonna Taylor, Ahmad Arbery, George Floyd, and others, many hip-hop artists released songs speaking out against police brutality. Many hip-hop figures took to the streets to protest or used their platforms to address injustice that harmed Black communities. Hip-hop artist Lil Baby released one of the most popular songs of 2020, "The Bigger Picture," days after protesting in Atlanta. "The Bigger Picture," which received two Grammy nominations, is a protest song that called for justice against police brutality in the United States and systemic racism. This song became one of the soundtracks during the protest, and it brought mainstream attention to the realities of police brutality and racism that Blacks face in the United States.

Further, hip-hop artists have been known to critique education systems. Au (2007) explains that "from the perspective of rap music, the discourse of education is largely dysfunctional when it comes to meeting the material, social, and cultural needs of African American youth." Popular hip-hop artists such as Dead Prez, Jay-Z, and Kanye West are known to critique school systems through their personal experiences. In their song "They Schools," Dead Prez critique American educational systems by suggesting that schools' curricula praise Europeans and offer negative views of Africans and African descendants. This highlights the lack of asset-based pedagogy that embraced and integrated the cultural identities and personal experiences of students. Hip-hop will always highlight and address injustices faced by the Black community. Through various mediums, including music, visual arts, dance, and technology, hip-hop, as a collective culture, acts against social injustice. The actions taken to raise awareness and dismantle oppressive systems are actions toward liberation. Hip-hop has a platform that reaches the masses.

Hip-hop exemplifies the power of liberation. It serves as a catalyst for positive social transformation. By integrating hip-hop into the curriculum, schools can provide students with an authentic platform to express their identities, experiences, and aspirations. Hip-hop educators not only embed hip-hop music into their curriculum, but they also support students in interacting with social change within and outside of their communities by creating projects and tasks that call communities to action, as hip-hop culture does. By leveraging hip-hop, we can foster critical thinking in *all* students (regardless of background). Additionally, it can bridge the gap between academic content and students' lives, making learning more relevant and engaging. By embracing hip-hop, schools not only recognize the cultural significance of this art form but also empower students to use their voices for advocacy and liberation.

Vibe Check

- **What challenges might you face when incorporating hip-hop into your teaching?**
- **Do you have personal reservations about you or others leveraging hip-hop culture for educational purposes? If so, what are they?**
- **How might using hip-hop culture impact your teacher identity?**

Hip-hop pedagogy encourages educators to recognize and highlight the brilliance, ingenuity, and creativity of hip-hop—a culture created by Black and historically marginalized communities—through curriculum choices and instructional decisions. Educators do not have to be experts in hip-hop culture, but they must work toward authentically understanding how their students engage and conceptualize hip-hop.

WHY HIP-HOP PEDAGOGY?

It's common for educators to fear judgment when engaging in teaching and learning practices that feel new or untraditional—especially those anchored in hip-hop culture. These fears may be grounded in negative perceptions of hip-hop culture, which reflect a lack of understanding of hip-hop—its ingenuity and connection to youth. These fears may be grounded in a belief that it is not an educator's responsibility to acknowledge their student's culture. These fears may be grounded in your interest in learning about your student's culture, but not knowing where to begin. At its core, hip-hop is a multimodal culture that provides various opportunities for participants to connect and engage with content. Depriving students of such learning experiences demonstrates a lack of understanding of your students and the responsive practices necessary for their achievement.

Hip-hop pedagogy is anchored in the creative elements of hip-hop, which is a cultural phenomenon that youth practice and engage in within their communities or access through media. Because hip-hop pedagogy is informed by hip-hop culture, it serves as both a culturally relevant way of engaging youth and as a way of incorporating multiple modalities within the instruction. Hip-hop pedagogy is beneficial for all students because it is derived from hip-hop culture, which naturally caters to every type of learner. Graffiti art activities allow students to make visual representations of concepts. The

MC inspired call-and-response provides an opportunity for students to aurally engage and learn concepts. Breakdancing activities provide students an opportunity to physically and kinesthetically move to gain a better understanding of science concepts. Thus, hip-hop pedagogy encourages visual, aural, reading/writing and kinesthetic learning styles (VARK) (Sankey, Birch, and Gardiner 2010). Fleming (2001) proposed that learners have a preferred learning style, namely, visual, aural, read/write or kinesthetic (VARK), with many students (about 40 percent) being multimodal (using a combination of these).

Hip-hop culture has impacted and empowered youth populations across the globe, especially youth of underrepresented groups, since its conception (Adjapong and Emdin 2015). Recognizing how inclusive hip-hop culture is to a variety of multimodal learners, it is easy to understand why hip-hop as a culture has transcended many other cultures and

Vibe Check

As an educator yourself, you may worry about some or all of the following:

- **What if I'm not familiar enough with hip-hop?**
- **What if my school administrators disagree with me including hip-hop informed practices in my classroom?**
- **What if parents are resistant to me incorporating hip-hop culture into my classroom?**
- **What if I don't know how to rap, dance, or do graffiti?**
- **What if I have too much content to cover and not enough time to incorporate these practices?**

undoubtedly influences young people who serve as its chief participants. To incorporate youth culture in schools, we must not only look at how and what young people are engaging in outside of school spaces, but we must learn to value it. Once we as educators understand the rich history and utility of hip-hop culture, we can then begin to value hip-hop as a culture. We can interrogate how hip-hop influences groups of people and, thus, leverage it as a conduit to making schools and educational spaces culturally responsive and equitable. Utilizing hip-hop pedagogy can provide you, the educator, with an opportunity to focus more on the cultural understandings of the youth and the communities you serve.

Hip-Hop Identities and Funds of Knowledge

Hip-hop pedagogy is informed by a sociocultural framework that explores the concepts of culture and social capital as they relate to the experiences of young people who identify as part of hip-hop culture. Vygotsky states, "human activities take place in cultural context, [and] are mediated by language" (John-Steiner and Mahn 1996, 191). Vygotsky asserts that we are never free of cultural influences. Even when engaging in action alone, cultural influences shape our thoughts and behaviors. The ways students dress, the ways they talk, the ways they dance, and the media they consume, as well as other nonverbal forms of communication, are informed by the cultures they experience both inside and outside of school. Many students' experiences outside of school are rooted in hip-hop culture (Emdin 2010). Once those practices are incorporated into teaching and learning, students are given the opportunity to engage in content as seamlessly as they would within their communities. I suggest bringing hip-hop culture into classrooms, not only by incorporating it into curricula but also by incorporating the culture into the ways in which teachers teach their students and into the overall school community. When classroom exchanges around content occur with the intentional use of hip-hop forms of communication, students use their funds of knowledge to engage with content because it's reflective of who they are (Lave and Wenger 1991; John-Steiner and Mahn 1996). Being culturally relevant through Hip-Hop Pedagogy not only allows students to view themselves and a culture that they value as a part of the classroom, but over time, it can also encourage independent self-education of content since students will take increasing responsibility for their learning (Ladson-Billings 1995).

In order to effectively teach and engage students, educators must be able to make connections between the global community, the content area, and students' local community, which in many instances can be different from that of the teacher. To function within a given culture, a person draws on a set of skills and knowledge that have been historically and culturally developed. These skills are called *funds of knowledge*. Scholars encourage the use of the funds of knowledge framework to better engage students across content areas (Barton and Tan 2009; González, Moll, and Amanti 2005; Hammond 2001; Moje et al. 2004). Integrating funds of knowledge into classroom activities creates a richer and more highly scaffolded learning experience for students. When an educator takes a step back from being a master of content and becomes a learner of their students' culture, experiences, and realities, it provides them with a unique opportunity to gather appropriate resources that are reflective and representative of students' experiences to use in the classroom.

Given the popularity of the music genre, the reach of hip-hop culture is broad. We all engage with it in a variety of ways, whether deeply or passively, and, as a result, possess a hip-hop identity. Some of us engage in hip-hop sensibilities in our homes, with our families and communities—hip-hop as a way of life—while others have a deep consumer-based connection to hip-hop culture. Regardless of how they connect and engage in hip-hop culture, most of our students have developed a fund of knowledge that allows them to successfully engage within hip-hop culture. Hip-hop pedagogues tap into their students' funds of knowledge and make connections to content areas to provide students with a learning experience anchored in their students' culture.

STRENGTHENING TIES WITH STUDENTS THROUGH HIP-HOP

Additionally, utilizing a pedagogy in a classroom that is directly anchored in the realities of students allows for the formation of social ties among members of your classroom community. A "strong tie" connects "friends" who have a lot in common. On the other hand, "acquaintances" who do not have much in common that would normally connect them share "weak ties" (Easley and Kleinberg 2010). Students need both strong and weak ties. Krackhardt (1992) describes a "weak tie" as "a 'local bridge' to parts of the social system that are otherwise disconnected, and . . . is likely to provide new information from disparate parts of the system" (216). When educators use a form of teaching that is directly connected to the realities and experiences of their students, then "weak ties"—a local bridge, that connects the students to the teacher—are formed, and the educator will be able to provide new information to the student. The reverse is also true. In turn, the student will be able to provide new information (hip-hop content) to the educator. The implementation of hip-hop pedagogical approaches involves the process of learning and utilizing the complex nuances of communication in hip-hop, which shows a valuing of student culture and allows for the creation of "weak ties" between the students, content, and even the educator (Burt 2001).

So what does this mean for you if you have reservations about utilizing hip-hop pedagogy because you don't feel you are hip-hop enough? It means that if you are enacting a pedagogy that is anchored in hip-hop, your classroom is serving as the catalyst to allow "weak ties" that already exist between you and your students to develop into "strong ties" over time. This means you are creating a space within the classroom where your students' "strong ties" can be expressed. Coleman (1988) refers to these connections as dense, close-knit networks that facilitate trust and cooperative exchanges. Nurturing these networks between you and your students, as well as among your students, can allow for a positive exchange of content. They provide a space for

> **Bringing It All Together**
>
> It never hurts to brush up on hip-hop history, even if you are familiar. But, if you're ready to dive into exploring your hip-hop identity, move on to the next section.

you to authentically learn about the realities of your students so that your classroom can be a space where learning occurs for both you and your students.

Lastly, it is essential to note that although students will be able to share key information about themselves, their preferences, backgrounds, and authentic experiences, it does not mean there is not work that is necessary for you, as the educator, to do on your own. This work includes having an understanding of hip-hop culture and history and remaining curious about hip-hop as it evolves.

A HIP-HOP HISTORY

Hip-hop is one of the most consumed genres of music in the world (Lynch 2018). However, many consumers of hip-hop music fail to recognize the rich history behind the birth of an innovative and progressive culture. Like many genres of contemporary music, hip-hop has roots in other musical genres, such as jazz, blues, rock, and funk, to name a few. Hip-hop, as we currently know it, was birthed in the Bronx, in the recreation room of an apartment building located at 1520 Sedgwick Avenue on August 11th, 1973, to be exact. Cindy Campbell, the mother of hip-hop, and Clive Campbell who is better known as DJ Kool Herc, the father of hip-hop, hosted a back-to-school party to generate income. This party brought the community together; young people and adults from the community all attended and DJ Kool Herc served as the DJ. Herc, a Jamaican native who moved to the Bronx as a child, was well known for spinning records in the community. He had a signature move as a DJ where he would find the break in a song, the moment when the vocals and most of the instruments that composed the beat would drop. Oftentimes during the break of a song, only the drums or bass line would be present, and DJ Kool Herc would prolong this moment of the song for the crowds' enjoyment. At the time, his signature move was called the *merry-go-round*. Today, it's most commonly known as the *breakbeat*. DJ Kool Herc developed his technique of playing only the breakbeat through observation and noticing that the crowd mostly enjoyed that part of the song, especially dancers who would commonly perform their specialty moves during the break. The breakbeat allowed space for a blend of talents to be presented. In the summer of 1973, in front of a large crowd, DJ Kool Herc's, technique of playing the breakbeat began a grassroots musical revolution, which is known to have birthed hip-hop.

If we took a closer look at the birthplace of hip-hop, the Bronx, in the 1970s, the elders of the Bronx community would recall a time when poverty was catastrophic, and violence over turf reached its peak despite efforts by the New York Police Department to penetrate local gangs (Chang 2007). It is important to note that these gangs that have been noted for committing violent acts against one another were also responsible for creating and organizing social events to uplift their communities despite economic and social challenges. Hip-hop was created as a social and therapeutic outlet (Emdin et al. 2016) by and for Black and Latino youth, many of whom were either immigrants or first-generation Americans, in response to the effects of industrialization in the Bronx (Chang 2007; Rose 1994).

The Breakbeat

The "Amen Break" is perhaps the most famous drum break of all time. It was performed by Gregory Coleman in the 1969 song "Amen, Brother" by the American soul group the Winstons. The breakbeat occurs from 1:26 to 1:33—the moment when all instruments except for drums are present. Rap producers in the late 80s rediscovered the track and have sampled the drum beat on many hip-hop songs including NWA's "Straight Outta Compton."

In the 1960s, the Bronx began to deteriorate as a response to increased challenges, including a steady rise in crime, a struggling economy, budget cuts to key social services such as the fire and police departments, and one of the largest construction projects that the Bronx borough has experienced (Gonzalez 2004). During the early

1900s, the Bronx was planned to be a suburban community, one in which people could conveniently travel a short distance to their jobs in Manhattan; however, during the 1950s and 1960s, crime across New York City rose dramatically, particularly in relation to drugs. Poverty was an underlying issue affecting many New Yorkers, but while the entire city experienced an increase in crime and poverty, the Bronx was hit the hardest. The increased crime rate encouraged many community members to relocate, especially those who were affluent and had access to the resources to relocate, which caused a significant change in the community as many homes, buildings, and commercial property became vacant (Figure 1–5) (Gonzalez 2004).

Robert Moses, a very influential city planner responsible for the construction of many New York City landmarks, including many New York City bridges, tunnels, and highways, was New York City's Construction Coordinator. Moses oversaw the development of the Cross Bronx Expressway. Popular thought was that this development would exacerbate the already devastating social and economic conditions of the Bronx and its community members. Caro (1974) suggests that the construction of the Cross Bronx Expressway is responsible for the downfall of the Bronx. Thousands of families were displaced and forced to uproot from their homes to allow for bulldozers, plows, and other construction machinery to pave the way for the Cross Bronx Expressway. Crime continued to rise in the communities that surrounded

Figure 1–5 • Abandoned building and car in a vacant lot in the Bronx

the Cross Bronx Expressway, which caused residents and businesses to relocate, deserting many buildings and storefronts.

In the midst of this social and economic crisis that plagued the Bronx, hip-hop music and culture were born in an effort to build strong communal ties. Urban youth organized and attended block parties to escape their unfortunate realities. Block parties, like the one hosted by DJ Kool Herc, Afrika Bambaataa, and the Ghetto Brothers (former street gang), created a space for young people in the Bronx to celebrate being young and free (Chang 2007). The power of music and camaraderie united Bronx youth, and "for the youth, the block party was the space of possibility" (Chang 2007).

Since its conception, hip-hop music has been and continues to be used as a tool to promote social justice. Hip-hop was about community and provided opportunities for young people, adults, and elders to gather, dance, and ultimately enjoy life regardless of the harsh realities that people in the Bronx faced. In 1982, the song perfectly entitled "The Message," by Grandmaster Flash and the Furious Five was released. "The Message" was the first hip-hop song to reach the television sets and radios of suburban America and it provided America with imagery of urban communities and the sense of frustration that people who lived in communities that seemed to be forgotten by society. At its core, hip-hop is a culture and genre of music that promotes social justice and provides an outlet for all to share their stories and experiences with the world.

Vibe Check

- What are some current songs, books, or media that express frustration or seem to serve as a voice for "communities that seem to be forgotten by society?"
- What are some ways to leverage these messages in the classroom or school community?

HIP-HOP HISTORY—THE MESSAGE ACTIVITY

The Message" by Grandmaster Flash and the Furious Five, released in 1982, is a historic song in the history of hip-hop and a powerful social commentary. This song is distinguished for its narrative style and focus on inner-city life's struggles and injustices. The song delivers a series of vivid verses that depict life in the inner city. The lyrics are a raw and poignant portrayal of the poverty, violence, and despair that were everyday realities in many urban neighborhoods. "The Message" is often credited with shifting the focus of hip-hop from party-centric themes to more socially conscious material. It opened the door for future artists to explore a wider range of topics and emotions in their music, making it a cornerstone in the development of the genre.

Watch the music video for the song "The Message." Consider the following questions to support in developing your understanding of hip-hop as a social justice movement

1. What themes are presented in the song?
2. Whose experience is being highlighted in the song?
3. Are the themes presented in the song relevant today?

Recommended Books to Learn More About Hip-Hop History and Culture

- *Can't Stop Won't Stop: A History of the Hip-Hop Generation* by Jeff Chang
- *The Hip Hop Wars: What We Talk About When We Talk About Hip Hop—and Why It Matters* by Tricia Rose
- *Decoded* by Jay-Z
- *Hip Hop America* by Nelson George
- *The Rap Yearbook: The Most Important Rap Song from Every Year Since 1979, Discussed, Debated, and Deconstructed* by Shea Serrano
- *Black Noise: Rap Music and Black Culture in Contemporary America* by Tricia Rose

Exploring Your Hip-Hop Identity

Hip-hop culture extends far beyond the bounds of music, permeating various aspects of our daily lives. Hip-hop is everywhere in mainstream society as its aesthetics, sensibilities, and influence are disseminated and absorbed by a broad audience. As a result, engagement with hip-hop culture shapes aspects of all our identities. Most people, even those who perceive themselves as distant from hip-hop, consciously or subconsciously, cultivate a form of "hip-hop identity." These identities exist on a spectrum, ranging from hip-hop spectators to hip-hop connoisseurs (Figure 1–6). They are not mutually exclusive and can overlap. Additionally, since our engagement with hip-hop culture can vary over time and context, our identities may shift accordingly. Hip-hop identities, like other identities, is dynamic.

> **Hip-Hop Spectator:** This identity includes individuals who may not actively seek out hip-hop music or culture but may be unconsciously influenced by it through mainstream media and societal trends. They are exposed to hip-hop through popular culture. They might not identify strongly

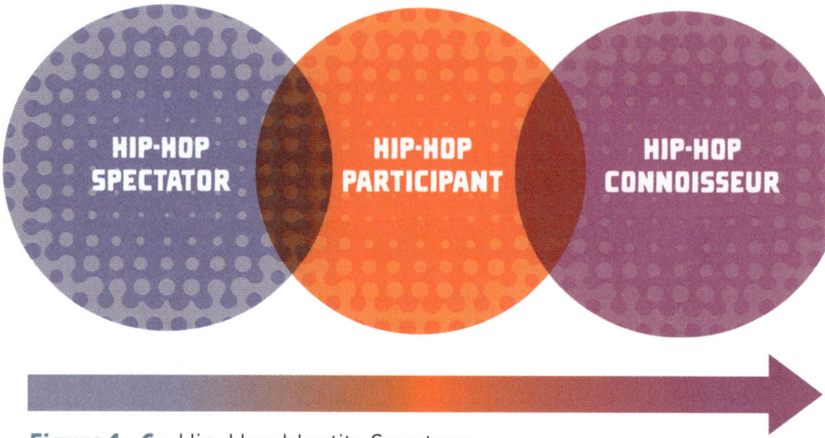

Figure 1–6 • Hip-Hop Identity Spectrum

with hip-hop culture or consider themselves fans. Hip-hop spectators may or may not recognize that hip-hop exists as a global phenomenon.

Hip-Hop Participant: This identity describes those who engage with hip-hop culture in a mainstream manner. A hip-hop participant might listen to hip-hop music regularly but may not necessarily delve deeply into the culture. Their engagement is centered around entertainment and enjoyment rather than a deep-seated cultural connection. They appreciate hip-hop as a popular music genre and are familiar with popular artists and hits but may lack an awareness of hip-hop history and/or cultural influences.

The Hip-Hop Connoisseur: This identity describes individuals who are deeply immersed in hip-hop culture. They are someone with a deep and extensive knowledge and appreciation of hip-hop culture and music. Identifying as a hip-hop connoisseur may involve recognizing an in-depth understanding and passion for various aspects of hip-hop culture. Hip-hop connoisseurs are often knowledgeable about the latest trends and news in the hip-hop community.

It's important to note that people from all backgrounds and with different interests can possess a hip-hop identity.

Hip-Hop Identity Reflection Questions

- Which of the hip-hop identities do you most identify with and why?
- Upon reflection of these hip-hop identity definitions, has your hip-hop identity shifted over time and in relationship to various contexts (geographic location, relationships, personal experiences, and so on)? How so?

YOUR ORIGIN HIP-HOP STORY ACTIVITY

Directions: Share your hip-hop story capturing a moment from your own life. Answer one or more of the prompts below.

- Describe your most memorable hip-hop experience.
- Describe the moment that you fell in love with hip-hop.
- Describe the moment when you realized hip-hop's influence.
- Describe the moment that you realized the educational potential of hip-hop.

2

Understanding American Historical Context to Become a Hip-Hop Educator

In schools and households across the country, we all, regardless of race and other social backgrounds, have been socialized to have inaccurate and negative perceptions of Black people. This socialization leads us to believe and accept negative and inaccurate views of Black people and other historically marginalized groups and creates biases. These biases then filter through our teaching practices and have detrimental effects on student outcomes. The systems, policies, and laws that uphold ideals of Black inferiority originate directly from America's history of chattel and racial slavery, which created white supremacist ideologies. In this chapter, you will gain an understanding of how laws and policies in American history—such as the abolishment of slavery, the creation of Jim Crow laws, and the ruling of Brown v. Board of Education—have been used to serve as proof of America's work toward Black liberation. These legal rulings and policies are often used in revisionist history today to demonstrate America's support for those who have historically experienced oppression. But in truth, the laws and policies only appear to work toward dismantling oppressive institutions. These pivotal moments serve as examples in American history where, despite an effort to make policy changes, American society chose to continue to uphold white supremacy, which significantly contributes to American socialization *today.*

As educators who teach in classrooms where the student body is becoming increasingly diverse, it is our responsibility to (1) develop our racial literacy, (2) reframe our teacher identity, and (3) interrogate positionality (Figure 2–1).

To deepen your understanding of the systems, policies, and laws that have upheld ideals of Black inferiority and their roots in America's history of chattel and racial slavery, you can read the following books:

- ***The New Jim Crow: Mass Incarceration in the Age of Colorblindness*** **by Michelle Alexander**
- ***The Warmth of Other Suns: The Epic Story of America's Great Migration*** **by Isabel Wilkerson**
- ***How to Be an Antiracist*** **by Ibram X. Kendi**
- ***Locking Up Our Own: Crime and Punishment in Black America*** **by James Forman Jr.**
- ***The Half Has Never Been Told: Slavery and the Making of American Capitalism*** **by Edward E. Baptist**
- ***Slavery by Another Name: The Re-Enslavement of Black Americans from the Civil War to World War II*** **by Douglas A. Blackmon**
- ***Stamped from the Beginning: The Definitive History of Racist Ideas in America*** **by Ibram X. Kendi**

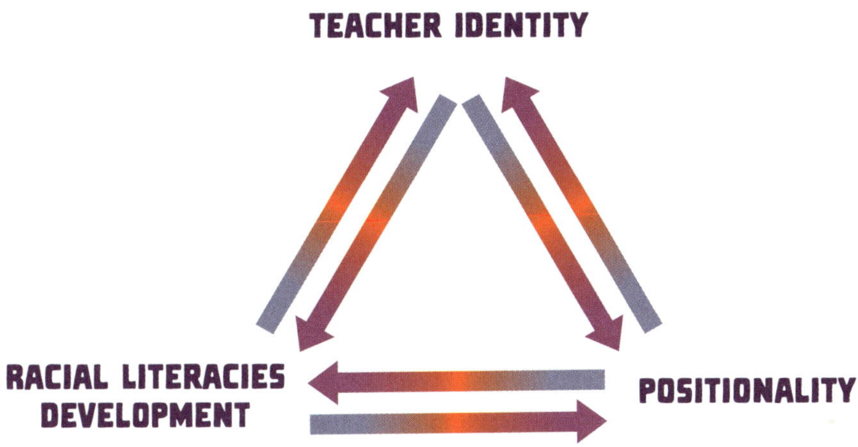

Figure 2–1 • A hip-hop educator is always interrogating their understanding of and placement in the world around them and of the communities that they serve.

THE ENTRENCHED LEGACY OF SLAVERY

In schools, students are exposed to literature and media that place America on the morally just side of history. We are socialized to believe that America was built on liberation and freedom for all. However, America was built on the *perception* of liberation and freedom for all. The reality is that Black people and people of color are still not truly liberated because racial inequities and injustices continue to persist, as they have always been ingrained in the fabric of our country since its inception. Our educational curriculum and our daily experiences with society and social politics uphold that America has been open to attempts to address social injustice. However, America has not demonstrated an eagerness to address its dark history and continuously supports efforts to minimize opposition against America's white supremacist legacy.

Slavery has always existed throughout the world, but America institutionalized the practice by making it a birthright for Africans and African descendants. Enslavement across Africa and Europe was not based on race, and enslaved people often had legal status and were eventually granted freedom and citizenship. Enslaved people in countries outside of America were able to buy back their freedom or were ultimately liberated by their enslavers after their period of enslavement. Therefore, the enslavement of groups did not last for generations because children were not usually born into slavery (Degruy 2017). In America, however, the institution of slavery evolved to be based on race and the convenient idea that African descendants were inferior. As a result, the perception that African descendants were inferior also grew, and they were considered "natural slaves" and "rightless persons" based on the color of their skin (Morris 1996). In 1808, though Congress banned the international slave trade, it simultaneously fostered a domestic trade system benefiting slave owners and the national economy under the guise of supporting Black liberation. In America, a land founded on liberatory ideals, children of enslaved people were born into a system that they could not escape nor would they gain any power within. This system developed into the institution of chattel slavery—a new practice that was used by Americans to "systematically turn the capturing, shipping, and selling of other human beings into a business, a business that would develop into the backbone of an entire economy, providing the foundation for the world's wealthiest nation" (Degruy 2017, 33). The United States, founded on principles of freedom, justice, and equality in 1776, contradictorily upheld slavery, as evident in its Constitution and practices. Despite these ideals, African descendants were enslaved and deprived of liberties. This contradiction was driven by economic motives to sustain the country's wealth. Consequently, because slavery predates most American institutions, institutions created during and after are inherently rooted in white supremacy and prioritize white dominance to the detriment of other racial and ethnic groups. At the heart of all institutions in America lives the legacy of the system of slavery and its birthed perceptions of Blackness, which we see persist through our social and political systems today, including education.

I often work with educators who doubt that educational inequities are directly connected to our socialized view of the Black community. Teacher preparation programs do not encourage educators to understand how America's historical contexts shape school ecosystems. As a result, educators may find it challenging to draw connections between the system and practice of slavery and how its legacy shows up in schools today through educational inequities, including culturally unresponsive curricula, cultural bias, school segregation, school funding, and discipline disparities, to name a few. Negative perceptions of Blackness that are birthed from the system of slavery are reflected in the way we interact with families and students across our educational systems.

As discussed in Chapter 1, integrating hip-hop and students' funds of knowledge into classrooms enhances learning by aligning with students' outside interests, fostering a comfortable environment, and encouraging independent learning through familiar cultural communication methods. However, this is not happening in most classrooms currently. As educators, we are trained to believe we should have complete control of the classroom. We often see ourselves as the holders of knowledge and students as empty vessels who should want to learn and receive it. Thus, we cement the belief that students must

Vibe Check

- How does this example in American history demonstrate a lack of remorse for Black people or those identified as inferior?
- How does this focus on America's economy question America's narrative around slavery?
- How do those in positions of authority remain empowered?
- How does this section combat American history's stance on its infant innocence and emphasize its intention to promote chattel slavery?

show up to classrooms in a particular way, i.e., not as themselves, so that they may receive knowledge from us and other deficit beliefs (Figure 2–2). In schools today, we contribute to the dehumanizing of students by not allowing and creating opportunities for the expression of self and culture and instead, demanding that students show up in ways that *we* deem appropriate and beneficial to their future success. As a result, white students benefit from the social structure of American schools because it reflects the same white supremacist culture that we are socialized into in society. This disproportionately and negatively affects Black and Brown students who may participate in a different culture at home. Those in positions of power and authority, including educators, continue to enforce ideologies, consciously or unconsciously, birthed out of the institution of slavery and the belief in white supremacy, which denotes those who are not

Examples of Common Deficit Beliefs in Education

- A student cannot achieve or will have a hard time achieving solely because of their circumstance
- Underprivileged students must work harder to meet the same outcomes as privileged students
- Parents do not care to be involved in students' education
- Parents buy students expensive clothing and sneakers instead of financially investing in their education
- Black and historically marginalized students benefit from "tough love"
- Students will not be able to handle lab equipment and classroom materials because they are expensive
- Students are not ready for rigorous or demanding texts or concepts

Figure 2–2

white as inferior to those who are white. Instead, educators must interrogate the various American systems that created the context for oppression so that we are mindful that we don't contribute to white supremacist ideals through our practice.

Vibe Check

What are some ways that you expect students to show up in schools that may be hindering self-expression?

Reflection Questions

- How do you reconcile the idea of America being founded on "freedom, justice, and equality" with the historical realities of slavery and its implications, as presented in the text?
- In what ways have you observed or experienced the legacy of slavery influencing educational practices and curricula?
- Reflect on a time when you might have unintentionally reinforced some of the deficit beliefs listed. How can you address and rectify this in the future?
- In what ways do you feel that the socialized view of "complete control" of the classroom impacts student–teacher relationships?
- How can you foster an environment that allows for the expression of self and culture, countering the dehumanizing aspects discussed in the text?
- How do you think the historical perception of African descendants as "inferior" or "natural slaves" affects the modern classroom dynamics and student–teacher relationships? Teacher–community relationships?

Jim Crow: An American Racial Segregation Campaign

As the sun set over the two-century-old institution of race-based chattel slavery within America, the sun rose on Jim Crow, a new institution that promoted racial segregation and consisted of policies and laws that would allow and encourage the continued oppression, massacre, and coercion of Black bodies across America. Jim Crow laws were any laws and policies created by states that enforced racial segregation in the South between the end of Reconstruction in 1877 and the beginning of the civil rights movement in the 1950s. The Reconstruction Era (1865–1877) brought about some positive changes for Black people in the South, including the expansion of the Freedmen's Bureau, which was charged with providing former slaves with basic necessities and introducing a public education system that provided an opportunity for many Black people to learn how to read and write. However, government intervention was necessary as Black communities faced challenges while integrating into white society. Thus, federal troops were deployed to southern states to support the enforcement of federal civil rights legislation. In response to federal government efforts of Reconstruction, the Ku Klux Klan used acts of terror and violence, including bombings and lynchings against local politicians and leaders, which resulted in the removal of federal troops from the south, thus abandoning Black communities seeking support as they fought to maintain their newfound freedom. The lack of federal and government support for newly freed Black people clearly supported the welfare of white people, which enforced slavery's ideology that Black people were inferior, "rightless people."

Jim Crow laws further systematized the segregation of people of color and Whites with the "separate but equal" decision of the U.S. Supreme Court in Plessy v. Ferguson in 1896, which upheld the constitutionality of racial segregation laws for public facilities as long as the segregated facilities were equal in quality. However, because we as a nation had already been ingrained in the perception that white people were superior to Black people, what was perceived as equal also became distorted. By the 1900s, every state in the South, as well as numerous states in the North, had laws and policies that discriminated against Black people and disenfranchised them in every sphere of life, including the deliberate separation of whites from people of color in public transportation, schools, parks, cemeteries, theaters, and restaurants. The doctrine that came to be known as "separate but equal" resulted in inferior facilities for Black people ranging from education to housing to employment. Jim Crow laws made it extremely difficult for Black people to participate in the electoral process, be elected to office, serve on juries, or participate as equals in the economic or social life of the South.

During the Jim Crow era, the legal system did not function in support of the upward mobility of Black people. Many former Confederate soldiers and supporters, fueled by the threat of losing their privilege and social status, worked as police officers and judges. This made it difficult and seemingly impossible for Black people to win court cases and subsequently ensured that they were systematically oppressed. Black Codes, another example of laws and policies that contributed to oppression, were local and state laws that restricted Black people's right to own property, buy and lease land, move freely in public spaces, and detailed when and how Black people could work. Black Codes forced Black people into indentured servitude, effectively removed their voting rights, and dictated where they lived. Despite the institution of slavery being abolished, the need to keep Black people in a place of inferiority persisted.

These beliefs and practices of the Jim Crow era have had lasting implications across institutions, which can be seen in schools today. For example, zero tolerance policies, which were originally designed to address severe behavioral issues, often result in suspension or expulsion for minor infractions, disproportionately affecting Black and students of color. Consequently, these policies often remove students from courses, further distancing them from opportunities to learn and contributes to the "school-to-prison pipeline," where students are pushed out of educational environments and into the juvenile and criminal justice systems.

Racial disparities, as a result of school discipline policies, are well-documented, with students of color, particularly Black students, more likely to face harsh disciplinary actions compared to their white counterparts for similar infractions. Additionally, the lack of a culturally responsive curriculum also contributes to racial disparities in schools. Examples of these are curricula that mainly focus on and reinforce Eurocentric views and perspectives and prioritize one group's experiences and achievements over others. Today, many schools across the nation face a concerning trend. Books and curricula that highlight, examine, and celebrate the experiences of Black individuals and communities are being banned. This suppression is driven by politicians and local school boards to ensure that all students are taught through a specific lens that overlooks the historical challenges faced by Black, Brown, LGBTQ+, and other historically marginalized communities throughout American history. The lack of culturally responsive curricula encourages the perpetuated cultural and historical biases that justified chattel slavery and were emphasized in Black Codes during Jim Crow. Some states have gone as far as dictating how topics, such as slavery, are introduced to students with nuance that suggests Black people benefited from enslavement. The deliberate enactment of policies and culturally unresponsive curricula are rooted in the ingrained idea and need to control or redirect Black people and are intended to police students and control what they learn in schools.

Brown v. Board of Education

In 1954, the Supreme Court of the United States of America identified that the "segregation of white and colored children in public schools has a detrimental effect upon the colored children" (Brown v. Board of Education 1954). This ruling effectively overturned the Supreme Court's decision of Plessy v. Ferguson of 1896, which upheld the constitutionality of racial segregation laws for public facilities commonly known as "separate, but equal." The Supreme Court's Brown v. Board of Education decision made it illegal to segregate Black and students of color from White students in public schools across the nation. As a result of the Brown v. Board of Education decision, White schools were forced by the federal government to desegregate and "accept" students of color.

The integration of public schools across America was immensely flawed. The federal government gave schools orders to integrate schools, but there was little to no direct support put into place or guidelines of best practices for curriculum and instruction or to ensure the well-being and general safety of all students, particularly Black students and other students of color. The Supreme Court ruled that school boards should proceed with desegregating schools with "all deliberate speed." Many Americans did not agree with the Supreme Court's ruling on desegregating public schools. As a result, individuals organized to prevent students of color from attending White schools. National stories of school desegregation, including the Little Rock Nine and the Boston Bus Crisis, provide details that illustrate the resistance that students of color faced from White communities when desegregating White schools (as shown in Figure 2–3).

Figure 2–3 • Elizabeth Eckford, one of the Little Rock Nine, was met by an angry mob on her first day of school, in a photo taken by an Associated Press photographer.

Vibe Check

Understanding all the historic moments discussed in this chapter, consider how the idea of "protecting" students comes up when discussing education inequities such as bathroom policies, banned books, migrant inclusions, and so on. Who is often protected, and who is often left to fight or fend for themselves?

Racism is deeply embedded in American social institutions. Institutional racism is distinguished from the explicit attitudes or racial bias of individuals by the existence of systematic policies or laws and practices that provide differential access to goods, services, and opportunities of society by race. We notice the consequences of this institutional racism across all social institutions, and education is no exception. The belief for many Black and families of color after the Brown v. Board of Education ruling was that their children and generations after would have access to quality education, more resources, and equal opportunities to meet high achievement rates. However, that is not the reality for Black and youth of color across America. The truth is that many youth of color still have their own traumatizing stories to share about their experiences with schools today.

Education researchers have studied the harmful effects on student academic achievement when students attend schools with fewer resources. Students of color make up the majority of students who attend schools with limited resources and, in turn, have fewer opportunities for achievement compared to their white counterparts (Kozol 1991; Necochea and Cline 1996). Further, studies show that urban schools, which mainly serve students of diverse racial backgrounds, have fewer experienced teachers, receive fewer resources, and teachers have less control over the curriculum, as compared to schools in suburban communities, which serve predominantly white students (Lippman, Burns, and McArthur 1996; Freedman and Appleman 2009). While the overall graduation rate in America hovers around 85 percent, the same is not to be said for Hispanic (80 percent), Black (78 percent), and American Indian or Alaskan Native Students (72 percent) (NECS 2023).

Chattel slavery, Jim Crow, and Brown v. Board of Education serve as a few moments within American History where America's response to Black oppression has been one that upholds white supremacy. As we interrogate laws and policies that were perceivably intended to support the freedom of Black people in America, we realize that the laws were not enforced and, as a result, in practice did not result in the full freedom and advancement of Black Americans. The lack of support and enforcement sends the message that the oppression of Black people would be tolerated and bolsters the notion of white supremacy. It is essential to note, however, that Black people have led the fight for their own liberation, freedom, and equality, which has ultimately also supported other race-based identity groups who have experienced similar forms of oppression. Hip-hop, in many ways, serves as a testament to the undying spirit and innovative brilliance of Black communities and their ongoing fight toward Black liberation.

Hip-hop culture was birthed to create contexts of love, joy, and liberation for Black and racially diverse communities. In this book, we will explore how educators can leverage Hip-Hop Pedagogy as a culturally responsive approach to teaching and instruction that engages and supports students in gaining an understanding of content knowledge and affirms students' culture within educational spaces. As with other culturally responsive practices, these strategies cannot be implemented outside of the context of examining the world critically. The hip-hop-informed strategies featured in this book cannot be implemented by educators without their acknowledgment of America's socialization and the historical oppression of Black communities. This oppression is what served as a catalyst for hip-hop's development and what contributed to its birth. So, before we dive into understanding how to leverage Hip-Hop Pedagogy as an approach to teaching and instruction, we must develop a teacher identity that encourages self-reflection and commits to unlearning biases.

The Journey of Becoming: From Awareness to Advocacy

It is crucial to understand the world around you when striving to become a culturally responsive educator. Maxine Greene (1978), a renowned aesthetics educator, theorized a philosophy of "wide awakeness," which she describes as maintaining a continuous sense of wonder, curiosity, and awareness about the world—which starts with self. Being "wide awake" means being critically conscious and fully present in one's experiences rather than going through life in a passive or unreflective manner. Green's philosophy of "wide awakeness" calls for educators to be fully engaged with the world, to question and reflect on their experiences constantly, and to imagine and strive for a better future. This requires the development of racial literacies, a deep understanding of the histories and social and political challenges of your school community, and constant and deep interrogation of your positionality. Wide awakeness insists on educators understanding their potential for personal and social transformation and confronting political and social challenges head-on rather than glossing over or ignoring them under the guise that they cannot be addressed within the classroom. Further, it encourages appreciation of differences and embraces the unique characteristics of every student, teacher, and school context.

Maxine Green's philosophy of becoming recognizes that the process of continual growth and development is an inherent part of the human experience. Becoming is not simply a linear process of moving from one stage to another but rather a dynamic and complex process that involves constantly reframing our identity, values, and relationship to the world. In essence, we are constantly becoming. As educators reflect and learn more about themselves and the communities they serve and become more open to being shaped by interactions with students and the broader school community, they will shift as individuals. Culturally responsive educators using Hip-Hop Pedagogy must strive to become wide awake and aware of social and political challenges plaguing the education system and school community, as well as constantly reframing their teacher identity to become better and more informed versions of themselves.

RACIAL LITERACY DEVELOPMENT IN THE CONTEXT OF HIP-HOP

Race is a social construct with no scientific or biological underpinnings, but it is used to categorize individuals based on shared physical, social, and cultural qualities. Earlier in this chapter, we examined how the societal concept of race and the labeling of Black individuals and people of color have resulted in them facing numerous forms of racial oppression throughout U.S. history. Today, we must acknowledge that the notion of race is not only deeply rooted in history, but it has fostered significant disparities, resulting in educational inequities. Racially literate educators can facilitate critical discussions around the content of hip-hop, unpacking complex themes of identity, resistance, and resilience. They can also employ hip-hop as a pedagogical tool to engage students in analyzing and critiquing societal structures, thereby fostering a classroom environment that validates students' cultural identities and experiences.

Dr. Yolanda Sealey-Ruiz defines racial literacy as an approach to examining racism and its impacts on social and institutional structures, such as schools (2021). Racial literacy is fundamental for a hip-hop pedagogue, given that hip-hop emerged as a culture focused on addressing racial inequities and empowering Black people. For educators, developing racial literacies is not a passive acquisition of knowledge but an active and ongoing engagement with the complexities of race and its manifestations in educational settings. It is about being capable of recognizing, discussing, interpreting, and challenging the myriad ways racial inequities are woven into the fabric of our school communities, including in our own practices.

Developing your racial literacy involves moving beyond a surface cultural appreciation to a deep, critical engagement with the cultural roots and contemporary expressions of students' identities. This process involves a myriad of steps, as Dr. Yolanda Sealy-Ruiz (2021) delineates in her robust framework, which encourages the promotion of both personal growth and systemic change.

Racial Literacy Development Components

Sealy-Ruiz (2021) identifies her racial literacy framework as the *Archaeology of Self*, which is about digging deep to unearth the foundational beliefs, biases, and experiences that influence how one perceives and interacts with the world, especially concerning race (Figure 2–4). The idea is that by understanding oneself better, one can identify areas for growth and address potential biases or blind spots.

The components of the Archaeology of Self: Racial Literacy Development Framework include critical love, critical humility, critical reflection, historical literacy, and interruption:

> **Critical Love** asks us to cultivate a profound ethical commitment to caring for the communities we work in, including caring for ourselves. *Critical love calls for more than just passive appreciation or acknowledgment for your student's cultures and identities. At its core, it underscores a deep-rooted commitment to genuinely caring for the communities that you and your school serve.*
>
> **Critical Humility** requires that we remain open to understanding the limits of our own worldviews and ideologies. *Critical humility is vital in this journey, acknowledging that educators' worldviews are not universal. This humility allows educators to appreciate the depth and complexity of hip-hop as a cultural expression and be open to learning from this vibrant art form.*
>
> **Critical Reflection** invites us to think through the various layers of our identities and how privileged and marginalized

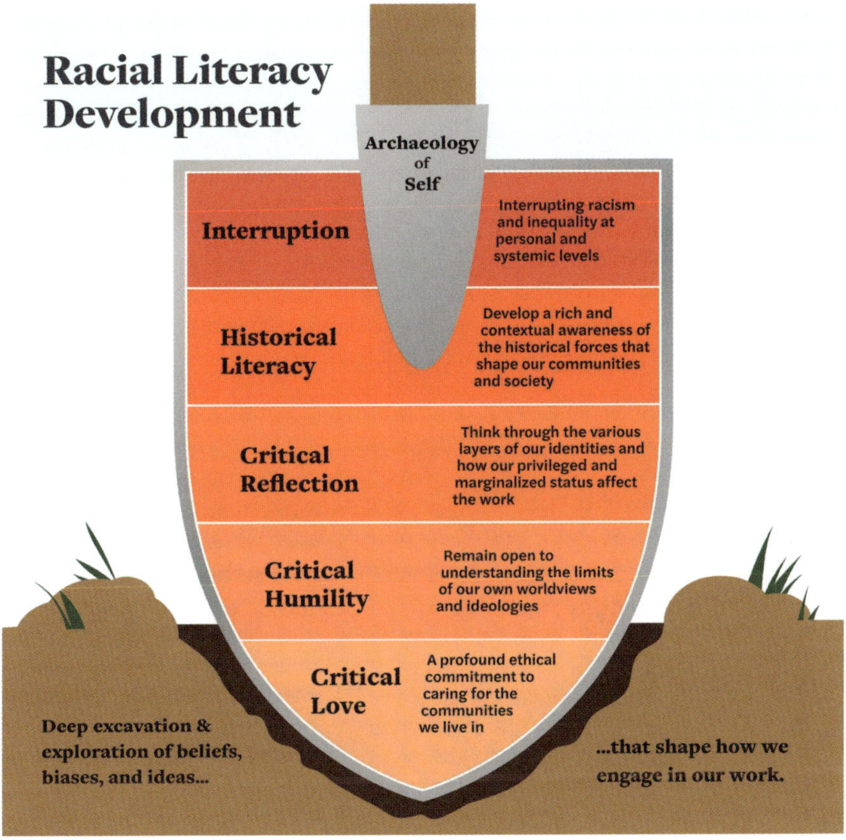

Figure 2–4 • Archaeology of Self Racial Literacy Development Model

statuses affect the work we do. *Critical reflection encourages educators to introspect their biases and privileges. Understanding these personal dimensions is crucial for an educator's ability to authentically engage with hip-hop culture and its social and historical contexts.*

Historical Literacy allows us to develop a rich and contextual awareness of the historical forces that shape the communities we work in and the society we live in. *Historical literacy is indispensable, particularly in understanding hip-hop's origins and evolution. A deep grasp of America's racial history informs a responsive and informed approach to incorporating hip-hop in teaching.*

Interruption is the point at which we interrupt racism and inequality at personal and systemic levels. *Interruption challenges educators to not only be aware of racial dynamics but to actively disrupt systemic racism. This involves advocating for change within the education system, ensuring that hip-hop, as a product of Black culture, is represented authentically and respectfully.*

For each of these components, I have identified an educator strategy and reflection questions. These are shown in Figure 2–5.

Racial Literacy Development Component	Educator Strategy	Reflection Questions
Critical Love	**Community Immersion:** Spend time within the community that you teach by participating in local events, or volunteering. This will provide an authentic understanding of the community's challenges, strengths, and dynamics.	How do you genuinely demonstrate your care and commitment to the communities that you serve in your daily interactions and teaching practices? In what ways do you actively seek to understand and connect with the lived experiences of your students and their families?
Critical Humility	**Foster Lifelong Learning:** Commit to being a lifelong learner, not just in one's discipline, but in understanding different cultures, perspectives, and pedagogical approaches. **Encourage Dialogue and Listening:** Create spaces where meaningful conversations can take place. This involves actively listening to students and colleagues, especially those who come from different backgrounds and have different perspectives.	What preconceived notions have you recognized in yourself regarding your students or their communities? How do you handle situations where your beliefs or worldviews are challenged, and how can you be more open to such challenges in the future?

Racial Literacy Development Component	Educator Strategy	Reflection Questions
Critical Reflection	**Journaling:** Keep a reflection journal to document experiences, reactions, and feelings concerning racial interactions or discoveries. This practice can reveal patterns in thinking and areas for growth.	How do the various layers of your identity (race, gender, socioeconomic status, etc.) influence your interactions and expectations in the classroom? In what situations have you felt either privileged or marginalized, and how might these feelings impact your approach to teaching?
Historical Literacy	**Interrogate History and Perspectives:** Begin with comprehensive books, documentaries, movies, podcasts, and visual art that cover racial dynamics in the U.S., then delve deeper with focused readings on specific events, policies, or periods. Prioritize works written by authors of color to ensure diverse perspectives. **Examine the Curriculum:** Examine your current curriculum. Are there gaps or biases? Advocate for and work toward a more inclusive and comprehensive curriculum that incorporates local community perspectives.	How well do you understand the historical contexts of the racial and ethnic groups in your classroom? What steps have you taken to ensure that your curricula and teaching materials reflect a rich and inclusive history? Where can you make improvements? What perspectives should be added to create a more inclusive curriculum?
Interruption	**Challenge Systemic Policies in Your Space:** Engage with school and department leaders to review and revise school policies that may contribute to systemic racism, such as discriminatory disciplinary practices or tracking systems that segregate students.	What are systems or policies in your school community that promote inequity? What can you do as an individual, staff, or school community to address systems/policies that promote inequity?

Continues

Continued from previous page

Racial Literacy Development Component	Educator Strategy	Reflection Questions
Critical Love	**Utilize Hip-Hop Pedagogy as an Educational Tool:** Hip-hop has deep cultural roots and is a powerful medium for addressing social issues. Use it in a way that respects its origins and conveys its messages of resistance and community empowerment.	How can you empower your students to recognize and challenge inequities, and how can you better advocate for systemic change?

Figure 2–5 • Sealey-Ruiz's Components of Racial Literacy Development (2021), Educator Strategies, and Reflection Questions

DEVELOPING YOUR TEACHER IDENTITY AND EMBRACING HIP-HOP IN EDUCATION

As you navigate the challenges and joys of the classroom, your teacher identity is shaped and reshaped. Through this evolving process, educators come to understand, define, and position themselves within the profession. This continuous reshaping of your teacher identity is crucial, as a strong, positive, and authentic teacher identity can lead to resilience and the implementation of more effective teaching practices.

Anyone who has spent a significant amount of time in America and/or has attended schools in America has been socialized to believe in and uphold white supremacy, either through values, ideals, or, most likely, subconscious beliefs. This socialization influences our identities as people and, more importantly, as educators—it's imperative to recognize, acknowledge, and interrogate this.

Regardless of who you are, your racial identity, your hip-hop identity, and your cultural background, if you desire to utilize hip-hop culture across educational spaces, you must develop a teacher identity that is conducive and responsive to the understanding and implementation of hip-hop across educational spaces. In order to reshape your teacher identity, you must reflect on what you have been socialized to believe and value, which means continuously working on developing competencies in racial literacies.

Vibe Check

Have you considered your positionality within your school's or community's context?

American Socialization and Implicit Bias in Teaching

Socialization begins before we are even born. We exist in a world with predetermined assumptions, rules, and roles based on our various social identities. At birth, we have ascribed identities such as gender, sexual orientation, religion, and class, to name a few—which initially are not our choice, nor do we have any control over. The spoken and unspoken rules of society direct us to follow predetermined norms. Throughout our lives, we are continually subject to various sources of socialization. Bobbie Harro (2000) describes the cycle of socialization and interrogates how socialization can promote the status quo of oppression within society and how we can interrupt the cycle and, in turn, interrupt oppression and oppressive systems. Harro's Cycle of Socialization (Figure 2–6) identifies the four key stages of this process: First Socialization, Institutional/Cultural Reinforcement, Additional Enforcements, and then potentially Disruption.

Our first socialization results from our interactions with our families or the adults raising us and with whom we spend a lot of time during childhood. Adults caring for a child prescribe the norms and rules that a child grows to follow. The people in a child's life serve as role models and model what is perceived by the child as "positive behavior." Because a child is dependent on the adults in their life, normally, children don't question the messages that are received from adults in their lives

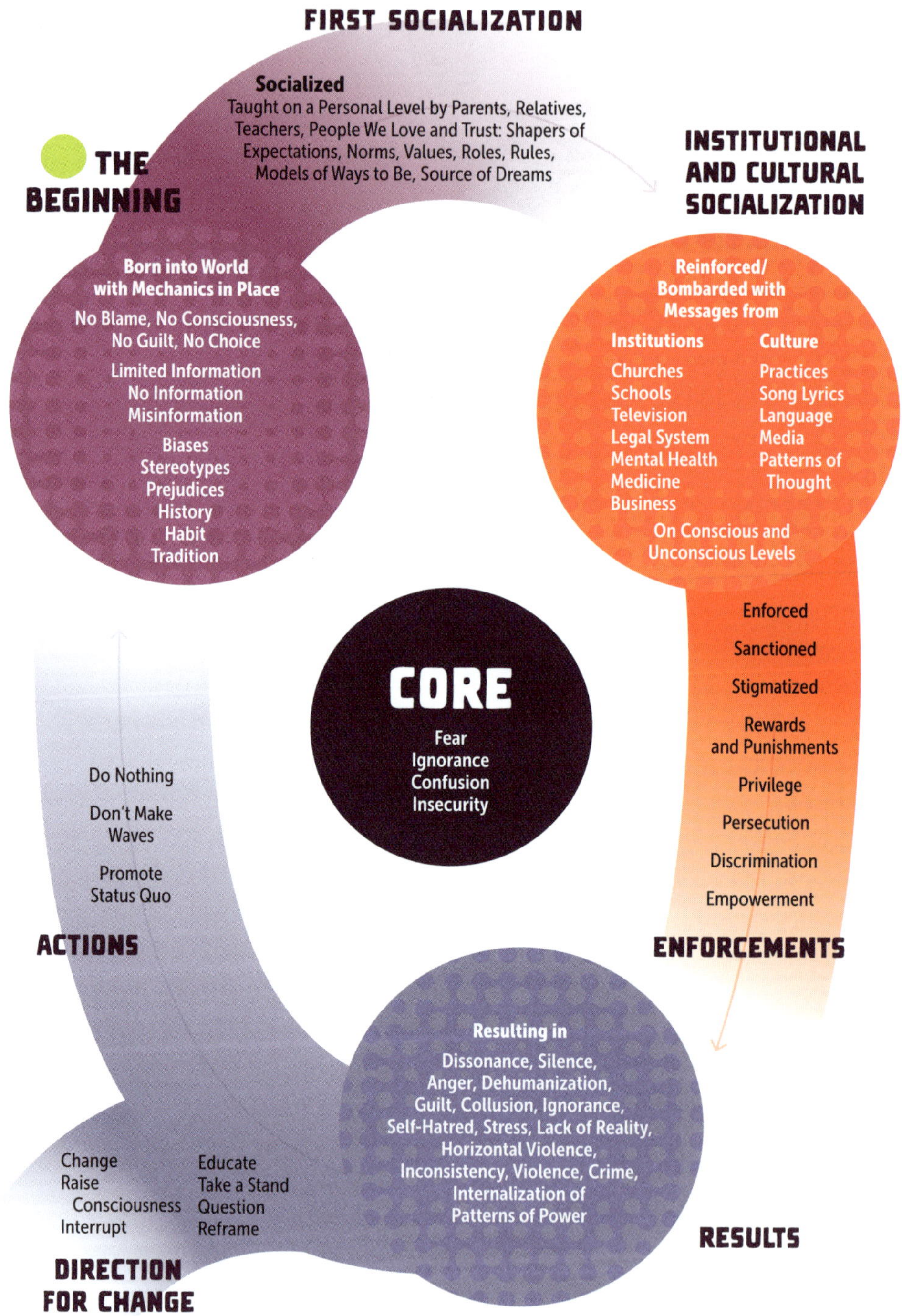

Figure 2–6 • Harro's Cycle of Socialization (2004)

and, as a result, unconsciously conform to their views and beliefs. This socialization happens intrapersonally (how we think about ourselves) and interpersonally (how we relate to others). Children are often told things like:

- "Boys wear blue, and girls wear pink"
- "Boys are supposed to like girls"
- "Girls are not good at math and science"
- "Christianity is the true religion"

Once a child begins to venture out into the world and becomes immersed in institutions and exposed to culture such as schools and media, the socialization caused by families and adults in the child's life is either reinforced or contradicted. At this point, we are inundated with social rules, roles, and assumptions within our society, which are unfair to both groups of people and people as individuals. The following are some examples:

- "Black people are more likely to steal from stores, which is why they are followed at higher rates"
- "Wealthy students have access to better schools"
- "White means good, and Black means bad"
- "Students in a classroom should follow order and be controlled in order for learning to take place"

While every child may not be raised to believe the aforementioned examples, these stereotypical messages are engrained and reinforced in American culture and often are unquestioned or challenged by children at a young age. We experience similar stereotypical messaging in all aspects of our society, including in media, music, and cultural practices, reinforcing our socialization. As a result, these messages ultimately shape how we think and what we believe about ourselves and others.

Stereotypical messaging and societal "norms" are well maintained within our society because there are enforcements in place to maintain them. We each have unique social identities that contribute to the messaging that we receive through socialization, which predisposes us to unequal roles in the system of oppression. When we are unaware of our socialization, we also reinforce these societal norms and stereotypical messages, which is why it's important to challenge and think deeply about our behaviors and how they may impact others.

There are often consequences when a person challenges a stereotypical message or a societal "norm." Often, a person challenging a societal norm is cast as a "troublemaker." Alternatively, those who conform, both consciously and unconsciously, to societal norms receive rewards and privileges for maintaining the status quo and may be regarded as an exemplary member of their group. Let's consider how this plays out in schooling using a fictional scenario:

> *Crystal is a socially active student who has a deep understanding of content, but she often roams around the class, calls out correct answers without raising her hand, and doesn't wear her school uniform. The teacher is often frustrated with Crystal and, as a result, disciplines her. Crystal sits next to Derek, who only speaks directly to the teacher and always raises his hand to participate but usually scores average on his content exams. Crystal is often disciplined for her social behavior, while Derek is praised for his. In this example, the teacher is socialized to perceive Crystal as solely disruptive and incapable of learning because of how she is choosing to demonstrate her knowledge, rather than understanding that various students may have different needs and modes of expression that contribute to various learning styles.*

This is how societal norms that reinforce negative stereotypes persist in our society. Although Crystal has a deep understanding of content, she may often be perceived as a "troublemaker" and/or "disruptive student," because the teacher fails to recognize and accommodate Crystal's modes of expression and learning style. We are often socialized to believe socially constructed messages about particular groups within society. There may be unchallenged narratives about Crystal that have followed her throughout her school career. Some beliefs about Crystal may be that she desires attention, cannot control herself, and likes to disrupt the learning of others. In reality, Crystal is actively participating in learning. Our belief in socially constructed messages often reinforce a bias that contributes to a negative perception of a whole group of people. Notably, although the teacher in the example is currently socialized to believe that a traditional, teacher-centered classroom is the best way of reaching students, through deep interrogation of oneself, a teacher can learn to expand their teaching style and become more equipped to teach through various learning styles in order to elicit knowledge from all students.

It is important to understand how our socialization contributes to our biases about various groups of people, especially as it relates to our students. Bias refers to the narratives and judgments we hold about groups formed through constant societal messages, stereotypes, and experiences. These repeated and often unchallenged narratives create automatic assumptions and reactions that can influence our behavior and decision-making without us being consciously aware of them. It is easy to identify explicit biases, but the more insidious implicit biases can still lead to severe consequences for students and have been linked directly to excessive discipline and lowered teacher expectations. Implicit biases are the unconscious attitudes or stereotypes that influence our actions and decisions without us even realizing it. These biases can affect our behavior and judgments in ways we might not be aware of, which is why it is important that we intentionally self-assess our implicit bias (Figure 2–7). We may explicitly endorse certain values, such as inclusivity, but may hold an unconscious bias that doesn't align with these values. For example, implicit bias might manifest itself in a teacher having a perceived notion that a student is dangerous because of their race. This will then affect the way the teacher engages with that student within the classroom, which may lead to the student not engaging in opportunities similar to those of their peers who are viewed as not dangerous.

Strategies to Self-Assess Your Implicit Biases

- **Take the Implicit Association Test (IAT):** Developed by researchers at Harvard, the IAT measures the strength of associations between concepts (e.g., race, gender) and evaluations (e.g., good, bad). This test can help you identify your unconscious biases.
- **Reflect on Past Decisions:** You can critically examine your past decisions, especially student interactions, grading, and/or classroom management. By reflecting on whether certain students were treated differently based on their race, gender, behavior, or other characteristics can provide insight into potential biases.
- **Seek Feedback:** You can ask colleagues or even students for feedback on their behavior and decisions in the classroom. This external perspective can highlight biases that may not be immediately apparent to the educator.
- **Implicit Bias Journaling:** Keep a journal to record thoughts, feelings, and decisions related to students. This practice can help you recognize patterns that may indicate bias. Regularly reviewing this journal can provide insights into your unconscious biases.

Figure 2–7

INTERROGATING EDUCATOR'S POSITIONALITY

Positionality refers to the relative social and political status in a given situation. Positionality is, by definition, relative. So it has to be considered in context. A person's positionality in their neighborhood is not the same as their positionality in a classroom, which is not the same as their positionality in a staff meeting. A person's race, gender, socioeconomic status, education, ability, sexuality, gender, religion, and cultural background, among other factors, contribute to their positionality. By understanding how positionality shapes perceptions and experiences, a teacher can approach issues of inequity and injustice with a more informed, empathetic, and critical perspective, ensuring that decisions and actions are inclusive and equitable.

Interrogating your positionality requires an examination and understanding of your own background, experiences, identities, biases, and how these factors might influence your perceptions, beliefs, and interactions. While interrogating your positionality requires understanding *who* you are, it also requires you to understand *where* you are. For example, a Black, American born female teacher teaching all Black students in a high school in the Bronx would experience a shift in positionality if they were to teach migrants students in Los Angeles. So, while who you are does not shift, where you are impacts who you are to others and your privilege in relationship to theirs. It is crucial for educators to understand how their positionality directly influences their teaching practices, curricula development, and interactions with students and families. Until this is done, a teacher cannot truly create an inclusive and culturally responsive educational environment.

Even if your identity matches that of your students, it is necessary for all hip-hop educators to constantly interrogate their positionality in relation to the context of the school community and students whom they serve and support. Hip-hop is a culture that is operationalized slightly differently across different social and geographical contexts. For example, rap music from New York is known for its classic boom-bap sound, characterized by heavy beats, sampling, and a strong emphasis on lyrical content. Compared to London rap music, also known as UK rap, which often incorporates elements of grime, drum and bass, garage, and dub, that reflects the city's diverse musical influences. Without an interrogation of positionality, educators risk leveraging hip-hop pedagogical approaches to maintain the status quo instead of creating educational spaces where students are able to critique oppressive systems and structures.

Black, Brown, and/or others who identify as part of hip-hop are not exempt from interrogating their positionality because they are also operating through their socialized perspectives of the world. It's important to reject the incorporation of hip-hop into schools only to the extent that it fits comfortably within the confines of white norms and values (Ladson-Billings 2013). To do this, we need to understand the ways in which hip-hop is often positioned as a singular thread, a curricular hook, or a simple pedagogical strategy that distances hip-hop from the Black historical traditions that birthed it. Instead, consider the incorporation of hip-hop in schools as a woven tapestry. Consider how you can incorporate hip-hop and Black historical traditions throughout your classroom, instruction, and school community.

Every educator who engages with hip-hop informed strategies needs to first understand how youth in their respective space engage, make sense of, and operationalize hip-hop before implementing any hip-hop pedagogical practices. Simply put, the innovation and new trends of hip-hop culture are created within Black communities, regardless of where they are acknowledged within mainstream media. Therefore, for educators to deliver authentic and effective hip-hop pedagogy, they must interrogate their positionality in relation to hip-hop populations that their students belong to (including but not exclusively racial identity).

To support hip-hop pedagogues in understanding how to interrogate their positionality as it relates to hip-hop populations, I draw from Milner's (2007) *Framework of Researcher Racial and Cultural Position* (Adjapong and Kelly 2023). Milner's framework provides steps for educators to process racial and cultural awareness, consciousness, and positionality and includes the following tenets: Researching the Self, Researching the Self in Relation to Others, Engaged Reflection and Representation, and Shifting from Self to System. I encourage all educators to work through the reflection questions in Figure 2–8 as a starting point for their own interrogation.

Framework Tenet	Description of Tenet	Guiding Reflection Questions
Researching the Self	Educators must engage in a critical reflection of themselves, which must include a reflection of their ideologies, beliefs, and practices in relation to the hip-hop population they are engaged with as well as the Black communities that create hip-hop.	• What is my experience with hip-hop culture? How do these experiences inform my teaching and research? • In what ways does my racial and cultural background influence the way I engage with hip-hop culture? • What do I believe about hip-hop culture? How do I negotiate my beliefs about hip-hop culture in my teaching and research? • What racialized and cultural experiences have shaped my research decisions, practices, approaches, epistemologies, and agendas?
Researching the Self in Relation to Others	Educators must examine themselves in relation to the hip-hop populations they are working with. This examination must center on the Black communities that created hip-hop.	• What beliefs do the hip-hop populations that I am working with have about hip-hop, and how might these beliefs shaped by their racialized and cultural lived experiences? • How do I negotiate and balance my own beliefs and interests around hip-hop with those of hip-hop populations I am engaged with, even if they are inconsistent with or diverge from mine?
Engaged Reflection and Representation	Educators must acknowledge and represent the voices and perspectives of the hip-hop populations they are engaged with, regardless of their alignment with the perspectives of the educator.	Educators should ask their students: • How do you engage in hip-hop culture (MC, breakdancing, graffiti, DJ, knowledge of self)? • How do you envision these aspects of hip-hop culture being demonstrated with our classroom community?

Continues

Continued from previous page

Framework Tenet	Description of Tenet	Guiding Reflection Questions
Engaged Reflection and Representation *(continued)*		Educators should ask themselves: • How can I authentically incorporate students' understandings and relationships to hip-hop in my classroom? • What would it look like to authentically incorporate students' understandings and relationships to hip-hop in my classroom? **Note:** Teachers should discuss pedagogical and curricular implementations of hip-hop with students after the learning experience to understand what went well and what should be modified in the future.
Shifting from Self to System	Educators must position themselves and their participants within the broader social, historical, and political contexts that hip-hop culture, education, pedagogy, and research exists.	• What barriers and structures—particularly ones that are systemic, institutionalized, or localized—impact my student population/school community? • How can I draw connections between curricular content and hip-hop praxis to interrogate institutional systems and structures that oppress specific groups?

Figure 2–8 • Milner's Framework of Researcher Racial and Cultural Position When Utilizing Hip-Hop in Education

3

The MC

The role of the MC is deeply connected with the history and evolution of hip-hop culture. Much like educators who curate and lead the learning experience in a classroom, the MC has historically served as the guiding voice in hip-hop, engaging audiences with powerful narratives, rhythmic delivery, and a deep connection to cultural roots. This chapter delves into the history of the MC, tracing its origins from the African griot traditions and Caribbean toasting to its pivotal role in the Black American church and the rise of hip-hop in the Bronx. As we explore the evolution of the MC from a supporting role to the central figure in hip-hop, we will draw parallels to the role of educators, encouraging you to embrace the identity of a Master of Content. Just as the MC has transformed the landscape of hip-hop, educators have the power to shape and inspire their students, using culturally responsive pedagogy to connect, engage, and empower. Through the conceptualization of the MC that I present, I encourage you to redefine your role, recognize your profound influence in your classroom, and consider how you can leverage this power to uplift and liberate your students, just as the MCs of hip-hop have done for their communities.

THE HISTORY OF THE MASTER OF CEREMONIES

Like an educator who serves as the formal host of a classroom space and learning experience, the Master of Ceremonies, also known as the MC or emcee, refers to the person who is serving as the formal host of a staged event, ceremony, or similar performance. When most people think of hip-hop, rap music comes to mind where a vocalist, or MC, rhymes over the sampling and mixing of beats provided by the DJ. Hip-hop was created by Black and immigrant communities who have inherent ties to African ancestry and the African diaspora. Currently the most popular element of hip-hop culture, the MC, has been associated with hip-hop culture and rap music since the 1970s and has a rich history with roots in Caribbean, West African, and Black American traditions.

In the 1960s, *toasting*, a style of lyrical chanting that involves a deejay talking over a musical rhythm, emerged in dancehall and reggae music from Jamaica. Toasts consist of comedy, storytelling, chants, and boastful commentaries. Although rhyming is not a requirement of an engaging toast, some toasts rhyme to capture the interest of an audience. Toasting became a popular part of musical entertainment as it provided another engaging layer of entertainment for an audience in addition to the dancehall and reggae music that was played.

The art of chanting over a beat or rhythm, arguably, did not originate from Jamaica. Music and vocalizing over a beat have long been a tradition of West African tribes and communities as far back as history can trace. Jamaicans carried West African ancestral traditions through generations, which evolved, inspired, and influenced the culture over the years. Toasting appears to descend from war chants and griot storytelling. Many West African tribes were known for their war chants. Warriors would chant over war drums to encourage motivation, inspiration, and confidence in preparation for battle. Music continues to play a key role in West Africans' daily lives through dance, healing, storytelling, and religious practice. A griot, master of oral traditions, is a West African storyteller, singer, musician, and oral historian. Griots originated in the Mande empire of Mali and, for centuries, have told and retold the history of the empire, keeping their stories and traditions alive over generations. West African griot tradition preserved history and played an integral role in West African society. In addition to being skilled orators, griots are known to be instrumentalists who trained and played various instruments that would act as the musical backdrop to their stories. Griots were viewed as leaders due to their positions as royal advisors.

The MC element of hip-hop is also heavily influenced by the Black church. Black preachers and clergy combine testimonials and parables in a way that engage the churchgoers and bring their sermons to life. A main tool of Black faith leaders (one which virtually all music historians and critics draw attention to in Black music) is the "call and response," in which the preacher calls out a sentence or phrase to which the congregation responds, creating a connection between speaker and audience. Call and response challenge the line between speaker and audience by encouraging a discursive form of public address, an open dialogue between preacher and congregation that makes the church service a spiritual and interactive experience for everyone alike.

DJ Kool Herc, the godfather of hip-hop, was born in Kingston, Jamaica, where he experienced neighborhood dancehall and reggae dance parties and witnessed the cultural phenomenon of toasting. It would be these experiences that contributed to the birth of hip-hop as we know it. DJ Kool Herc and his family migrated from Jamaica to the Bronx at the age of 12. DJ Kool Herc brought his cultural and community knowledge and experiences gained from Jamaica—his country of origin—to the Bronx, which was integral to the conception of hip-hop as we know it today.

The Evolution of the MC

During the early days of hip-hop, before it became a global phenomenon, the DJ was an central element of hip-hop culture. DJs had large followings, and their names were always prominent on party promotional items, with the MC's name listed less prominently. The DJ was the center of attention and the MC's initial role was to introduce the DJ and to get the crowd excited for the DJ's set. Over time, the best MCs refined their craft and found ways to engage the crowd by rhyming during their introduction shows and providing commentary during block parties. MCs chant and rhyme over beats, telling stories, shouting out prominent members of the community, and providing fun and engaging rhyming commentary while the DJs play their set (Figure 3–1). As hip-hop evolved, so did the MC's role. The most popular DJs and most popular MCs teamed up to host trendy parties and community events that combined the two skill sets.

Figure 3–1 • Grandmaster Caz of the Cold Crush Brothers performing (as both DJ and MC) at Roosevelt High School in the Bronx, 1981.

Today, when the average person thinks of hip-hop, hip-hop musicians, and notable MCs like Jay-Z, Megan Thee Stallion, Nipsey Hustle, and Doechii, to name a few, are what come to mind. But this wasn't always the case. The focus of hip-hop culture shifted from the DJ to the MC as hip-hop became popular with audiences worldwide. Released in 1979, Sugar Hill Gang's song "Rapper's Delight" is credited with introducing hip-hop music to a wide audience outside of New York City. The song reached the top music charts in the United States, United Kingdom, and Canada. As hip-hop music became more popular during the 1980s and 1990s, it also became commercialized. The core element of the MC continued to evolve to become a more prominent fixture in hip-hop culture, and as a result, the role of the MC also evolved. DJs took a backseat, and the focus shifted to the MC and what they had to say. The role of the MC shifted from being a party host who would encourage the crowd to be excited for the DJ to an artist who performs their own lyrical content to an audience. MCs focused on making studio records that appeal to the general public to garner national and international attention. Now, in hip-hop, an MC, who is more commonly known as a rapper, is a music artist who creates and performs original lyrical content.

Over time, MCing has become synonymous with rapping. Though hip-hop's commercialization encouraged the role of the MC as the center, it did not change the role of the MC as personal and narrative storytellers, critics of systems, and structures that promote social injustice. The MCs continued to spread their messages with the goal of inspiring and entertaining their audience.

As MCs became increasingly popular, they also got more creative with their performance techniques and use of their platforms. The MC, whose role was to initially provide supplementary entertainment, has evolved into one that provides a global platform for hip-hop to birth leaders, entrepreneurs, and community activists. I highlight a few contemporary MCs who have used their identity as an MC to have a larger impact in communities and that transcend hip-hop culture.

Jay-Z has always been iconic and pushed the boundaries of hip-hop since the release of his first album, *Reasonable Doubt,* in 1996. Like many artists, Jay-Z was hustling for a record label deal to support the release of his first album, but when no such deal materialized, he, along with a few friends, decided to create their own record label called Rocafella Records. Rocafella Records grew to be one of the most notable record labels in hip-hop history. In the essence of growing your own, throughout his career, Jay-Z started a clothing brand, liquor company, music streaming service, and sports management firm, and through a few of these business ventures, he was able to drive his status and influence as a rapper to new heights. In 2018, Jay-Z became hip-hop's first billionaire, with his steadily growing kingdom that encompasses business deals in art, real estate (homes in Los Angeles, the Hamptons, Tribeca), and stakes in companies like Uber. Jay-Z used the influence gained as an MC to delve into and leverage successful business deals throughout his career. Jay-Z is also known to advocate against issues of social injustice by involving himself and his legal team in several legal cases involving Black men who have been mistreated by law enforcement. In a guest column in the Hollywood Reporter, Jay-Z reflected on his desire to amplify discussions around issues of social justice and his decision to produce documentaries about Kalief Browder and Trayvon Martin, Black boys who lost their lives in response to the abuse of law enforcement (Carter 2017). Jay-Z's influence gained as an MC has allowed him access to spaces and opportunities that might not have been afforded to him otherwise, demonstrating the power and influence of hip-hop as a culture.

Bringing It Full Circle

Jay-Z is leveraging his fame, influence, and resources to amplify the voices of those who have been historically marginalized and silenced, exemplifying liberation as he challenges the power dynamics that typically suppress these voices, allowing the stories and struggles of these individuals to reach a wider audience. This amplification of historically marginalized voices disrupts the status quo and pushes back against systemic oppression.

Similarly, Megan Thee Stallion, a Houston-bred MC, leverages her music and platform to advocate for women, specifically Black women. In a New York Times op-ed, Megan shares her personal experience as a victim of an act of violence and calls for the public to support and respect the voices and experiences of women (Stallion 2020). Megan's music explicitly displays women's sexuality without centering men. As an approach to intersectional feminism through her music and influence, Megan shares sexualized images of women to highlight important issues that negatively impact women. For example, in her music video "Thot Shit," Megan highlights the efforts of Black women across all essential industries as well as society's lack of appreciation and respect for the work and commitment of Black women. As an MC, Megan has leveraged her sexuality to reclaim power both in her performances as a rapper and also as an influencer of her generation. She promotes body positivity and calls out mainstream society's idea of one acceptable body type. Identifying as an activist for women's rights, Megan leverages her influence as an MC to evoke positive change in the hip-hop community.

Also committed to social activism before his untimely death in 2019, Nipsey Hussle's deep commitment to his community continues to be carried on through his legacy. The Los Angeles–based rapper's brilliance was in his ability to be an MC, community advocate, and entrepreneur all at once. Operating on a scarcity model, he produced

Bringing It Full Circle

- Megan Thee Stallion's open expression of her sexuality is a powerful assertion of her agency and exemplifies joy, love, and liberation.
- Megan Thee Stallion exemplifies joy by fully accepting and celebrating her sexual power as she reclaims control over her body and how it is perceived, countering the societal tendency to shame or police women's sexuality. This reclamation of agency is a profound act of joy, as it embodies the freedom to be oneself without fear or apology.
- Megan Thee Stallion's demand for higher expectations for how Black women are treated in hip-hop exemplifies love for the community. By challenging the oversexualization of Black women, she calls for a deeper recognition of their humanity, talent, and contributions. This demand for respect is an act of love, as it seeks to protect and uplift Black women within the culture, ensuring they are valued for more than just their physical appearance.
- Megan Thee Stallion's open and unapologetic expression of her sexuality exemplifies liberation. By reclaiming her sexuality on her own terms, she challenges the historical objectification and exploitation of Black women's bodies. This reclamation turns what has often been a source of control and oppression into a source of power and agency.

a limited amount of his first mixtape *Crenshaw* and sold copies for a premium of one hundred dollars each. Selling a mixtape for one hundred dollars, especially as a new artist, was unheard of in hip-hop, as artists generally want their music to reach the masses. He understood his value as an artist and wanted to share his perspective and appreciation for entrepreneurship with his community in Crenshaw, Los Angeles. Throughout Nipsey Hussle's career, he encouraged Black people to be entrepreneurs and highlighted injustice found and experienced within inner-city communities in his music. More importantly, he was an advocate for the very same community that raised him and created various opportunities for those who have been pushed to the margins of society. Hussle is an exemplar of what all educators should strive to be in their communities and within their classrooms. As someone who was once affiliated with a gang, he often spoke about his experiences with gang culture and police brutality. Hussle sought to create solutions for community members who were negatively affected by gang violence. Los Angeles Police Commissioner Steve Soboroff, shared via X, formerly known as Twitter, that he was scheduled to meet with Nipsey Hussle to discuss gang violence and ways to support young people who come from neighborhoods that often have ties to gangs.

Bringing It Full Circle

Nipsey Hussle's decision to sell his mixtape for one hundred dollars was a statement of self-worth and a reflection of his high expectations for himself as an artist, which exemplifies love. This confidence wasn't just about personal gain but also about challenging his community to recognize and support the value of hip-hop culture. By setting a high price for his work, Nipsey was essentially saying that his art—and by extension, the art and culture of the hip-hop community—was worth more than the industry typically acknowledged.

Hussle used his platform as an MC to advocate for his community and, at the time of his death, was in the process of creating solutions to address gang violence. Hussle also advocated for STEM education by investing in Vector 90, a co-working space and STEM center located in the Crenshaw district that is dedicated to addressing the lack of diversity in the science, technology, engineering, and mathematics fields. As educators, we can choose to carry on the legacy of Nipsey Hussle by empowering students to advocate for themselves and each other demonstrating a love for themselves and their community.

Doechii, an openly bisexual artist, consistently demonstrates her support for the LGBTQ+ community through her music, public statements, and personal experiences. Her music incorporates themes of self-discovery and acceptance. Her breakout track "Yucky Blucky Fruitcake" reflects on her exploration of her sexual identity. During Pride Month 2024, she shared a heartfelt letter highlighting the love and acceptance she has received from LGBTQ+ fans. She wrote, "I owe a tremendous amount of gratitude to the LGBTQ+ community for embracing me so tightly and pushing not only my music but also championing my personal growth." These reflections underline her recognition of the community's role in uplifting her career and reinforcing her personal journey.

Doechii has also spoken about the challenges of navigating the hip-hop industry as a queer artist. In interviews, she has described how the LGBTQ+ community provides her with a sense of safety and understanding that she does not always find within hip-hop. Her advocacy extends to collaborations like "Alter Ego" with JT, a former member of City Girls, where both artists celebrate self-love and encourage others to seek spaces of support and acceptance.

Through her music and advocacy, Doechii has established herself as a voice for LGBTQ+ inclusivity and representation. As a prominent up-and-coming hip-hop artist, Doechii's openness about her identity and her gratitude for the LGBTQ+ community is inspiring but also challenges hip-hop's norms, paving the way for more diverse voices to thrive.

The MC in hip-hop is much more than just a rapper or hip-hop artist. Hip-hop is the most consumed genre of music and a multibillion-dollar industry that offers MC platforms and opportunities to leverage their influence for positive social change. The aforementioned MCs are a few examples of MCs who have an impact on hip-hop culture through their commitment to addressing social injustice through their obtained platforms. Just as there are MCs who are intentional about supporting communities, there are MCs who do not identify as activists

Bringing It Full Circle

Doechii's support of the LGBTQ+ community exemplifies joy, as she embodies the transformative power of hip-hop to affirm her multiple identities. Doechii's openness about her bisexuality and her intentionality in uplifting LGBTQ+ individuals demonstrates joy as she expresses herself authentically and unapologetically. By exploring her own sexual orientation in songs like "Yucky Blucky Fruitcake," she not only validates her own experiences but also provides a sense of belonging for others who may see themselves reflected in her lyrics.

and who are not interested in harnessing their influence to better their communities. Similarly, educators have influence within their classrooms and can choose to leverage their classrooms to address social injustice alongside their students. However, it is the choice and responsibility of the educator to create opportunities within their curriculum to interrogate social injustices and how they impact students' local and global communities.

MC AS THE MASTER OF CONTENT

In hip-hop, the responsibility of the MC is to cater to the needs of their audience through entertainment. *MC* acquired backronyms such as "microphone checker," "microphone controller," "music commentator," and one who "moves the crowd" through their lyrical content. As we draw connections between the MC and teaching, I propose a new backronym that considers educators as the MC, or the Master of Content. Just as the MC is a central component of hip-hop culture, educators are central to education. Similar to the MC in hip-hop, an educator's most important responsibility is arguably to attend to the cultures, needs, and interest of their students.

In Chapter 2, we explored the importance of understanding your socialization, positionality, and biases. In this chapter, I invite you to take your introspection a step further and work on reclaiming your power as an educator. Throughout history, MCs have redefined their role and reimagined it so it may benefit them personally and their community and advance hip-hop culture as a whole. The role of the MC has evolved from solely introducing DJs and other acts during a hip-hop party to the MC being a solo act in curating and creating music that is listened to across the globe, as well as performing and commanding large crowds at hip-hop shows. I encourage educators to redefine their role and reclaim the power that is associated with identifying as an educator. Educators must recognize how their social position and power shape their identities and, as a result, how they are perceived by society (Ambrose et al. 2010). Educators have the power to teach, impart content knowledge, facilitate understanding, develop skills, and serve as mentors to young people. We can focus on the negative public perceptions of teachers, or we can consider how we, as educators, can have an effective and lasting influence on the students to whom we are dedicated to serving.

Educators train for years to gain a deep understanding of teaching strategies, curricula development, assessment strategies, and their selected content areas. To this point, I encourage educators who strive to be culturally responsive in their practices and mindset to identify as MCs—Masters of Content. Even after years of higher education, an effective educator is always *learning*, always *growing*, always *becoming*, always *evolving*. Additionally, a Master of Content uses Hip-Hop Pedagogy's conceptualization of love to set high expectations for themselves and their students. They invite and honor how and when joy reveals itself and do so to support the liberation of their students and communities. For this reason, I identify Masters of Content as educators who strive to be culturally responsive in their practices and mindset by engaging and implementing Hip-Hop Pedagogy. Masters of Content are not only experts in subject areas such as science, math, English, social studies, and so on, but in their approaches to teaching and learning, as well. Masters of Content also commit to aligning their mindset, teaching philosophies, and practices to culturally responsive education and are able to reflect their personal identities and inspire learning in the classroom.

Masters of Content understand:

- how to draw connections between content knowledge and students' lived experiences
- how to use the context of students' communities in their instruction
- how to read a classroom to collect informal data from their students
- how to assess the needs of various students
- when to interject during a class discussion and when to step back and allow students to process and make sense of content practice skills
- to always center students' needs and experiences.

While there are many backronyms for MCs that we accept, there is one that hip-hop pedagogues reject: Master of the Classroom. Master of the classroom refers to an educator who facilitates a teacher-centered classroom where the teacher has the primary responsibility of communicating knowledge to students in a learning environment (Mascolo 2009). This traditional, unidirectional form of teaching and learning is not empowering or engaging to students. Masters of the classroom center the teachers' experiences and ways of constructing knowledge while providing little to no consideration for students. While masters of the classroom may be active, their students are passive. Passive learners are compliant and are driven by the completion of tasks, answering recall questions, and memorization—these skills serve as primary assessments of knowledge and indicate examples of a teacher-centered classroom. A master of the classroom does not demonstrate love, joy, or liberation in their practice because they believe the teacher must be centered for true learning to take place. Conversely, a Master of Content initiates love, joy, and liberation to create opportunities for students to apply knowledge, discuss and negotiate meaning, and create change in their community because they believe students already have the capacity to do so *within* themselves, not because of the teacher.

Masters of Content work alongside students to gain a deep understanding of students' needs and experiences. In hip-hop, while an MC may be at the forefront of the crowd/audience, in order to be effective at captivating and connecting with the audience, they must consider, understand, and respond to the needs and desires of that audience. Similarly, the responsibility of an MC as an educator is to position themselves as constant learners of their students and gain insight of students directly from students—not their perception of students. This work requires creating a space conducive for students to make sense of their needs and experiences. Moreover, the learning environment should invite students to bring their authentic selves into the space, which functions as joy. This is the only way to gain an authentic and accurate understanding of students and then leverage these understandings as assets within the classroom.

As with hip-hop MCs, Masters of Content have core responsibilities that are all centered on the benefit of their audience and their students: know yourself, know your power, remain persistent, and remain authentic. We will explore each of these responsibilities in turn.

Know Yourself

As stated in previous chapters, a Master of Content must recognize that their culture and personal experiences influence their attitudes and shape the way that they view the world. Every person has implicit bias that shapes their actions, understandings of others, and decisions. Regardless of whether your students' cultures differ from yours or if you identify as part of the same culture and background as your students, it's important to be sensitive and open to understanding the difference in attitudes and ways of engagement. To create a culturally responsive classroom, a hip-hop educator needs to be aware of their actions and work toward shifting their mindset to being inclusive, open minded, and accepting of the differences of others. This will create opportunities to learn about the cultures of your students and their communities, which will inform your sensitivity when engaging and responding to the needs of students and their communities. Further, creating opportunities for students to uncover and interrogate their own implicit biases supports an inclusive classroom.

Know Your Power

Masters of Content recognize one of the realities of the profession of teaching is that they will always face challenges and critiques from the general public, but still make the decision to focus their energy and attention on ensuring that their students' needs are met by exhibiting love, joy, and liberation in their practice. Masters of Content make the decision to reclaim the role and power of the educator by creating classroom contexts that celebrate and empower young people through the facilitation of learning. Masters of Content recognize that the work may be overwhelming because larger systems may be at play. However, they do not let these systems undermine the decisions they do have control over, such as how they approach grading, what questions they pose their students, which texts they bring into their lessons, and which projects they use to assess student learning.

Additionally, Masters of Content actively work toward becoming a better version of themselves as they assess their own behavior, engage in reflective practices, listen and respond to students, and are real with themselves about where they may be in their own journey. Masters of Content recognize that they will always be working on *becoming* so that they may gain a deeper and more nuanced understanding of others' experiences as time progresses. This empowers the Master of Content and allows them to see their role and power as one that strengthens with time.

Remain Persistent

Though the Master of Content incorporates new understanding of students' cultural backgrounds and individual needs when planning for instruction and the establishment of the classroom environment, they also know that trial and error is part of the learning process as well. A Master of Content acknowledges that there may be times when the implementation of new ideas may fail, and despite this, they will continuously find ways to persist and experiment with new practices until they receive the intended response from students and communities.

No one educator will have the power to single-handedly make all changes necessary to meet all the needs of students and their communities. The goal of knowing all students well is to use that knowledge to create better, more inclusive teaching and learning opportunities that align with students' cultures, interests, and needs. Masters of Content decenter themselves in the classroom and create opportunities to learn about the different cultural backgrounds and interests of students directly from students because they understand that their generation of students will change over time. What worked with one group of students one year may not work the next. Understanding students as individuals is also important, as students who identify from similar backgrounds still have their unique interests. Establishing informal and formal check-ins with students, whether one-on-one or in small groups throughout the year, will help you learn about the unique needs of students. Students may feel comfortable talking about themselves in smaller groups or individually if a relationship has already been established between teacher and student. At the end of this chapter, you will find examples of these strategies.

Remain Authentic

Though the hip-hop MC is widely praised for their raw and detailed storytelling abilities, MCs have gained tremendous influence based on what their audience perceives as authentic. Hip-hip music accounted for 22 percent of all music sales in 2020 (Eser 2024). Hip-hop is a multibillion-dollar industry and as a result many people try to participate in hip-hop culture solely with the intention of profiting. With hip-hop moving from the margins of mainstream popular culture to the focal point, the culture that birthed hip-hop music evoked the concept of authenticity to protect itself from the perils of commercialism (McLeod 1999). Thus, remaining authentic as an MC is vitally important, regardless of your background. As long as you stand in your truth and are true to yourself, your culture, and your community, hip-hop will accept you. This is because hip-hop was created to be an inclusive culture that provides a space for contributions from various and multiple identities.

This desire for authenticity is shared in the classroom. Like with the hip-hop MC, authenticity is key to being an effective culturally responsive educator and Master of Content. Authentic educators are willing to share appropriate details of their lives and display elements of their humanity by telling personal stories, making jokes, and admitting mistakes. Authentic educators demonstrate compassion and care toward students by recognizing them as individuals and creating opportunities to listen to their needs and perspectives (Johnson and LaBelle 2017). As educators, many of us are trained to separate our personal lives and identities from our professional careers—not to divulge any personal information to students out of fear that they will somehow use it against you. I'm not advocating that educators divulge every detail of their personal lives to students, but making efforts to share curated and appropriate aspects of your personal life will humanize you to your students and greatly impact how students perceive you. Research demonstrates that students report higher levels of learning and a deeper understanding of learning experiences they described as authentic. By teaching authentically, teachers may create more meaningful experiences and deeper learning for all students in a variety of settings and across disciplines (Johnson and LaBelle 2017). Ultimately, just as they pay attention to an MC's ability to remain authentic, students pay attention to the messages educators send about themselves in the classroom. When educators are authentic, share aspects of themselves, are empathetic, and consider the needs of students, there are increased opportunities for positive relationships to be established between students and educators, as well as increased opportunities for deeper learning. Authenticity is a critical component of meaningful communication in multiple contexts, especially in the classroom.

Learning to Listen and Not to Judge

MCs contribute to hip-hop by sharing their stories to provide social insight into their realities. Sometimes, these realities are problematic and highlight the many challenges facing the hip-hop community. Additionally, there are MCs and record label executives who exploit problematic narratives for profit. Though these narratives may lack depth and authenticity, students may find interest and connection with them. Our goal as educators and Masters of Content is to learn to listen and understand why without judging.

Society loves the image of a hip-hop artist toting guns, glorifying violence, and inciting fights regularly. They love to see a hip-hop artist that magnifies negative stereotypes of the hip-hop generation—this image of hip-hop feeds directly into White America's racially biased perception of urban and hip-hop youth. White folks, the largest consumer group of hip-hop, who generally participate in hip-hop culture solely by consuming hip-hop music, have a limited understanding of what hip-hop culture fully is. Rather than doing the necessary work to learn more about a culture that is not original to them, they use their limited understanding of hip-hop culture to make sense of the realities of Black Americans and members of hip-hop culture. Hip-hop is a medium where people from historically marginalized communities and groups can share stories of their realities, and it includes the identities of millions of its followers across the globe. It is not fair for consumer-based hip-hop to emphasize a narrow narrative of what hip-hop is. Consequently, we must consider the effects of this one-dimensional narrative on participants' and consumers' perceptions of hip-hop culture and Blackness. Further, as educators, we must create space within our classroom to have open dialogue and be critical of media, including hip-hop, that students consume every day. Creating this space begins by learning to listen and respond to our student's interests, even if they may not be interests of our own.

LISTENING AND RESPONDING TO STUDENTS

Schools are created to serve students, but students have the least amount of input in the school decision-making processes and how they are educated. Adults make most, if not all, of the decisions that affect schools and, in turn, the school community, including students. Students have helpful information that can inform school policies, culture, and instructional practices and can help educators gain valuable insight into their various identities and learning styles. Further, students' input can support educators in creating more equitable classrooms.

As an educator, you spend most of your day with students, and during that time, you are intrinsically learning things about students. If you have the skill of being attentive, you may learn what motivates, upsets, and brings joy to students. Through assessments, you may understand what academic support and intervention students need to develop skills and competencies. Some educators are naturally skilled at listening to and understanding students to support them in engaging and building positive relationships with students, but many are not. Most educators' understandings of students come from their implicit biases and experiences with similar students, even siblings of students that they have taught throughout the years. Each new group of students that you teach every year is different. Each individual student that you engage is different. Each student in your class sees the world differently because of their culture, personal experiences, and community upbringing. Not creating opportunities to listen to students ignores these facts and assumes all students are the same. Students have various learning needs and social emotional needs that need to be understood by the educator to create a culturally responsive classroom. Many educators may believe that having a positive rapport with students means they are culturally responsive, but we cannot assume that a positive rapport between students and teachers equates to students sharing their voices and insights or even effective teaching practices. While daily interactions with students and the resulting insight educators gain from students can inform practice and policy, this is not enough. When educators make a conscious decision to listen to students, they can garner specific insight that can be used to tailor decisions about text selection, approaches to key concepts, and seating and group arrangements, to name a few.

I have worked with educators who argue that there is no need to create structured opportunities to listen to students because they have taught in a particular school context for years and "know it all" when it comes to students and/or they are from a similar cultural or racial background of students. Educators who do not see the value of creating structured opportunities to listen to students do not recognize or value students' individuality. Further, these educators make assumptions about students based on their past experiences and implicit biases. Even if a teacher has taught in the same community for over a decade, students change over time. Influenced by technology and life events, student needs today vastly differ from those of the previous generation, hence the importance of a Master of Content's ability to evolve.

A critical aspect of a culturally responsive classroom is the teacher's ability to genuinely listen and respond to students to create a classroom environment that is inclusive and reflective of the needs and desires of all stakeholders within the classroom space. In hip-hop, the MC has a responsibility to listen, respond, and cater to their audience. An MC's fans and audience empower the MC, and the MC feeds off this energy to provide a relatable product and/or performance. In hip-hop and Black culture, the power resides with the people and never with a singular person. Likewise, with effective listening and responsive practices, the students empower the teacher by providing authentic feedback to inform the educator's practice. The truth is that students decide how much a teacher can influence the classroom and what they can do with that power. In a classroom where the teacher does not listen to students or provide opportunities for student feedback, the teacher has a false sense of power that is enshrouded in compliance and, sometimes, fear. If an MC is not responsive to the needs of their audience, they will lose influence over their audience. If an educator does not create opportunities to listen and respond to students in the classroom, they will lose their students. Students may physically be in the classroom, but effective teaching and learning cannot occur. Without student inclusion, effective teaching and learning are not active or long-lasting. In hip-hop, the audience leaves energized and inspired by their interaction with the MC. In the same way, students should leave their classroom feeling invigorated and ready to apply new skills and knowledge in their lives.

The Cogenerative Dialogue

As an MC, educators must create structured opportunities to listen and respond to students. Moreover, students need to understand that they are being heard and that their insights will be used to create positive change that benefits them and their community. One such approach is having *cogenerative dialogues*. A cogenerative dialogue is a form of structured discourse in which teachers and students engage in a collaborative effort to help identify and implement positive changes in a classroom's teaching and learning practices. Through engaging in cogenerative dialogues, teachers and students co-develop strategies for instruction that focus on the students' socioemotional and academic needs. The dialogues enable open communication concerning both the teacher's and students' perspectives on schooling (Emdin 2016).

A cogenerative dialogue is a formal conversation between a small group (4–6) of students and an educator with two purposes: (1) to gain authentic insight into students' experiences, identities, and needs and (2) to identify solutions to issues of classroom culture and instruction. The cogenerative dialogue creates an opportunity for structured communication among stakeholders of the classroom community with the goal of creating an understanding of participants' varied identities, needs, and experiences, as well as identify solutions to improve student and teacher experiences. The teacher needs to plan, prepare, and follow a protocol to implement an action plan based on the cogenerative dialogue. During the cogenerative dialogue, students and teachers are viewed as equals, and students should be encouraged to talk freely but respectfully about their experiences in the classroom and how specific classroom issues should be resolved.

When engaging in structured approaches to listening and responding to students, like a cogenerative dialogue, students may not always initially respond positively. It's necessary to recognize that students have navigated schools that have not genuinely acknowledged their cultures or considered their voices and authentic perspectives for most of their lives and may be skeptical of the initial attempts of the educator to listen to students. As an educator, you can demonstrate that students' opinions are valued by prioritizing student voice and using student feedback to inform your practice and classroom culture. In time, students will come to realize their voices have an impact and may even begin to look forward to these dialogues.

Many students appreciate when a teacher or adult genuinely ask for their opinion or feedback. But they may not always feel comfortable enough to share it. Level the student–teacher power dynamics by setting up opportunities to be available to students outside of class time to provide students with the space to express their voice. Be open to feedback, particularly around seating, student tasks, grading policies, classroom policies, and texts. Pay particular attention to how students interpret your choices in class as well as your tone, pacing, and grading. In cogenerative dialogues, some students may suggest isolating students who may not show interest in academics in the same ways, they may suggest removing classroom policies that may be conducive to learning and offer structure. The idea of a cogenerative dialogue is to take student feedback that will support the learning for all students and to demonstrate to students that you are willing to try their suggestions with fidelity. Taking student feedback and implementing it is a necessary step toward building relationships with students that develop trust and the ability to exchange ideas and develop learning environments where students feel comfortable taking academic and intellectual risks.

Co-Teaching: Students as MCs

In hip-hop, when an MC is performing for an audience, the lead MC is often accompanied by a fellow MC (hype man/woman) whose essential role is to support the lead MC. For a hype man/woman to be effective, they must have a deep understanding of the musical content of the lead MC. Co-teaching with your students provides the opportunity for them to showcase their mastery of the content while serving in the role of a hype man/woman in support of the lead MC (the teacher), and ultimately supporting their peers in gaining that same level of mastery.

Through co-teaching, the teacher and students will be able to work collaboratively to engage students in content. The goal of implementing this approach in a classroom is to allow the responsibilities for instruction to be shared between the two professionals. For this strategy, the student is identified as a professional and expert in the classroom. As the responsibilities for instruction are shared between both the teacher, who is normally viewed as the main authority figure of the classroom, and the student, the student feels a sense of empowerment and excitement that can allow them to take responsibility for their own learning and participation to enhance their, for example, science content knowledge.

Identifying Student MCs

We all have natural MCs in our classrooms. Sometimes, we call them the alphas of the class or instantaneously recognize them as the students who are most charismatic. Sometimes, they are the most academically inclined students and other times, they present themselves as the offbeat class clown. These are the students who have a seemingly natural command of the class' attention on most, if not all, days. Identifying these students and celebrating their gifts will support a Master of Content on their journey to co-teaching with students. Identifying the MC can elicit critical insight into what's working in the class and what requires attention.

Figure 3–2 shows the four key steps to identifying your co-teachers and leveraging that relationship to uplift your students.

The Path to Co-Teaching with Students

1. Share intent
2. Recognize diversity of students (not only racial/ethnic diversity)
3. Note social command
4. Be a hype person for your students

Figure 3–2

First, be honest with your students about your intent in finding fellow MC(s). While monitoring student progress in a lesson, be attentive to how your potential MCs may be communicating with other students. What and how do they communicate feedback, directions, or next steps to their peers? Are they condensed? Do they offer models? Do they use a particular word or type of language, such as comparisons and analogies, to make themselves clear or explain a concept? Do they use humor to make a point? How do their peers receive this type of communication? Be curious about your MC's crafty communication style.

Next, recognize your MCs are not one-size-fits-all. True to its Jamaican origins, the MC may be reflective of a student who is rhythmic with words, funny in nature, or charismatic in character. Ironically, the student you may initially believe to be the MC may not be appropriate for the role or may not want to do it. You may also be inclined to select a natural student leader whom you already have a relationship with. It is important to note that part of identifying your MC requires recognizing any bias that may surface, such as believing one student being better equipped to step into the role than others. Masters of Content acknowledge that the student MC may not necessarily be a student they are naturally inclined to build a relationship with.

Then, recognize your MC's powerful social moves. Take notes on how your MC moves socially in the school. In what ways does the MC leverage their influence? Do they hype up another MC? Do they hype up multiple students at once? Are they usually keeping to themselves and quiet, yet use their mystery and intellect to persuade the crowd into taking action? Or is the MC comical, whimsical, and swift with questions? Do they adapt to situations or problems creatively? Or do they draw in their peers with attentive listening? Either you instinctively recognize and attempt to leverage the MC's abilities, or you must work hard to gain the trust of your MC to successfully establish an inviting class culture. Failing to do so may mean isolating groups of students from the class environment and therefore furthering achievement gaps within the locus of your control.

Hype up your MC. Some MCs may know their influence and how to use it, while others may not. Let them know you recognize their strengths. Name them and how they contribute to the classroom or school community. For example, you could say, "I noticed that when you participate in a group discussion, you ask questions that offer the opposite perspective. I appreciate this because it allows students to consider different points of view."

As you aspire to become a hip-hop educator, I encourage you to embrace your role as the Master of Content, recognizing your immense power to influence and uplift your students. Just as the MC in hip-hop curates content that resonates with the audience, your task is to deliver culturally responsive and engaging lessons that reflect the diverse identities, needs, and experiences of your students. By knowing yourself, understanding your power, remaining persistent, and staying authentic, you can create a classroom environment that fosters love, joy, and liberation. Like the MC who moves the crowd, your influence as an educator extends beyond the classroom, shaping the minds and lives of your students. It is your responsibility and privilege to ensure that every student leaves your classroom feeling empowered, heard, and inspired to apply their learning to make meaningful changes in their communities and the world.

Graffiti

Graffiti art holds profound significance as the visual arts component of hip-hop culture. In this chapter, we explore the origins of graffiti art, tracing its roots back to the streets of Philadelphia in the 1960s, where it began as a form of personal expression and evolved into a powerful medium for social commentary and resistance. We examine how graffiti, birthed from historically marginalized voices of inner-city youth, transformed public spaces into vibrant canvases that challenge social inequities and reclaim identity. As educators, understanding the historical and cultural context of graffiti allows us to see its potential as a tool for promoting creativity, critical thinking, and cultural pride in our students. This chapter highlights how graffiti art can be leveraged within educational settings to support students' self-expression and engagement with their communities, ultimately helping them connect with their own cultural backgrounds and develop a sense of belonging and agency.

THE HISTORY OF GRAFFITI ART

Graffiti art, characterized by its vibrant colors, intricate designs, and bold statements, has emerged as a powerful visual medium that intersects with hip-hop culture as its visual arts component. Modern graffiti, as we are familiar with today, started in Philadelphia in 1965 by Darryl McCrary, known as Cornbread (shown in Figure 4–1). During the 1960s, many inner-city communities predominantly populated by Black people, including Philadelphia, experienced long-standing grievances regarding police insensitivity and brutality, inadequate educational and recreational facilities, high unemployment, poor housing, and high prices, which led to outbreaks of violence across the United States. While growing up in this environment, Cornbread, a teenager at this time, wanted to get the attention of someone he was interested in and tagged "Cornbread Loves Cynthia" on a Philadelphia building.

We see tags of aliases on walls, lockers, bathrooms, desks, or, my favorite spot to find graffiti art, in textbooks that will be used for years to come. Passed down for years before a school is able to provide newer, updated text, and an intention for many opportunities for viewership and interaction, textbook graffiti art offers what buildings and New York City subway lines offer—long-term and expansive visibility.

Figure 4–1 • Darryl McCrary, aka Cornbread

The rise of graffiti art in urban areas marked a clash between young artists like Cornbread and local governments who viewed this artistic expression as vandalism. Marginalized youth used graffiti as a form of defiance and to voice their struggles, transforming public spaces into expressions of identity and protest. Government and local police efforts worldwide aimed to eradicate graffiti, fearing urban decay and negative public perceptions. Heavy fines and increased surveillance targeted artists, promoting a narrative of criminality.

Though his initial motive was gaining the attention of a love interest, Cornbread continued to tag his name in public spaces across Philadelphia as response to the social conditions that he experienced within his inner-city community. As he tagged his name on buildings and objects across the city, he gained recognition from people within his community who were intrigued and began talking about the new phenomena of graffiti-painted walls. The more people spoke about Cornbread, the more enticed he was to tag his name in a new public space and community members soon began to recognize his tag. He describes tagging as a way of "involving myself in the neighborhood," as opposed to being involved in selling drugs or participating in gang wars. "I wasn't about that," says Cornbread (Mass Appeal 2016).

GRAFFITI ART AS A RESPONSE TO SOCIAL INEQUALITY

Although graffiti's intent did not begin as a social political one, the art form served as a type of artistic expression for groups that have historically been denied opportunities for expression within mainstream artistic platforms due to entrenched inequalities. Graffiti art provided youth from historically marginalized communities with a powerful means to reclaim public spaces within their communities and voice their concerns and respond to social inequity, urban decay, and political unrest. The public display of artistic expression grew in popularity because it served as a response to conditions created by a lack of sufficient social programming and a lack of access to art programming, institutions, and museums. Artists reclaimed their voices, turning walls into powerful visual narratives that confront systemic injustices. Graffiti art has also been widely used as a tool for protest and to express political opinion.

> **Bringing It Full Circle**
>
> Graffiti artists use their artistry to draw attention to and highlight social issues in their community which communicates their fight toward liberation.

Urban decay and neglected inner-city communities, like the Bronx, played a crucial role in the emergence of graffiti in New York City. Deteriorating infrastructure, such as abandoned buildings and vacant lots, created visually unappealing neighborhoods, contributing to a feeling of neglect and abandonment by community members. White flight, the phenomenon of white people moving out of urban areas, particularly those with significant racially diverse populations, in addition to the economic disinvestment in historically marginalized communities, further perpetuated neglect and limited access to public resources. In response to the deterioration of urban communities, such as the Bronx, New York City implemented initiatives by urban planner Robert Moses, who was known as New York's "Master Builder." Moses led the construction projects of many roadways, bridges, and tunnels across New York City, aiming to rejuvenate neighborhoods by renovating apartments and establishing space for commercial enterprises such as shops and restaurants. However, reaping the benefits of these plans necessitated the displacement of vulnerable community members from their homes, often resulting in the demolition of their residences to make way for new roads and structures. As a result, this process contributed to the dismantling of low-income and racially diverse communities. Instead of providing support to struggling communities, it paved the path for gentrification—the coerced relocation of vulnerable inhabitants, a decline in affordable housing availability within urban centers, and the exacerbation of economic inequality. These urban renewal plans directly relate to the oppressive cycle of disadvantaging Black and Brown communities while simultaneously creating an advantage for others.

While Moses' infrastructural projects were focused in New York State, his philosophy of urban development influenced a generation of engineers, architects, and urban planners across the United States. This would lead to adverse impacts on urban communities across the

United States. Community members were allowed little to no input in how the urban renewal plans were actualized and, in turn, how the plans would affect the local community. This voicelessness exacerbated community members' sense of abandonment and frustration and robbed them of agency. The forced displacement, inequitable policies, political unrest, and rising social tensions further contributed to the climate of discontent and protest that existed in urban communities and provided inspiration for marginalized communities to seek avenues for self-expression.

In this turbulent economic and social landscape, graffiti artists utilized their resources and creativity. They used deteriorating buildings and subway cars as blank canvases to reclaim public spaces within their community and to assert their presence in response to policies that literally pushed many community members out of their homes. With the use of vibrant colors and intricate designs, artists transformed public structures into symbols of resilience and pride. Through their graffiti, artists addressed pressing social issues, critiqued societal inequalities and demanded attention to the needs and concerns of their communities. Graffiti art quickly became a platform for visual protests and social commentary within inner cities across America, empowering individuals to challenge the existing norms and advocate for change. Understanding the social and political context in which graffiti emerged is essential for

Bringing It Full Circle

The use and intentional placement of graffiti artwork on visible and public spaces exemplify sentiments of the artists' love for their community. While they simultaneously acknowledged local government's abandonment of their community, the artists worked toward changing and beautifying their environment.

Graffiti art exemplifies joy as it promotes of self-expression, community pride, and cultural resilience. Graffiti is an art form that allows individuals to assert their presence and identity in public spaces where they may otherwise feel invisible. Graffiti art is about claiming space, which is inherently joyful, as it reflects a celebration of one's existence.

recognizing its significance as an artistic movement deeply rooted in the struggles and aspirations of marginalized populations.

Though graffiti's beginnings were in Philadelphia, Cornbread's innovation quickly spread to other major cities. In New York City, graffiti took off as a popular art form amongst youth during the 1970s. As with Cornbread, the originating idea behind graffiti—finding platforms to express freely, be rebellious, and paint whenever and wherever one pleases—appealed to young people because it offered them an opportunity to publicly display their creativity and identities. Subway cars were the initial and prime target for tagging because they were moving canvases. As subways moved throughout New York City, there were more opportunities for artists' work to be seen by the public. As the art form grew in popularity, graffiti artists rose to the challenge to make their tag names stand out. The objective became to tag up popular public spaces to showcase art that reflected the identities of artists and would be viewed by many. Simple tags evolved into large, colorful, and elaborate pieces, and new font styles were developed, such as wildstyle (Figure 4–2a), stencil (Figure 4–2b), block letters (Figure 4–2c), and bubbles (Figure 4–2d). As artists' visions for their tags became more complex, they also grew in size.

Eventually, it became the norm for New York City subways to display full art pieces that took up the entire length of the subway car. The increasing visibility of graffiti art in mainstream culture highlighted its artistic value. This led curators and art galleries to begin to recognize the cultural and artistic value of graffiti art and expression. Art galleries that were not accessible to youth due to a lack of social programming and funding began to open their doors to curate art shows to display graffiti works of art. The work of iconic artists like Jean-Michel Basquiat and Keith Haring played a pivotal role in elevating graffiti to the realm of "high art." Their success and rapid rise to fame challenged the idea that graffiti was a destructive act and led some cities and communities to experiment by designating controlled public spaces where graffiti art could be created and displayed legally. The recognition from galleries elevated the status of graffiti artists and paved the way for the acceptance of street art as a legitimate and valuable form of artistic expression.

Figure 4–2a • (left) *Wildstyle* is a highly sophisticated form of graffiti lettering. It features letters that intertwine, overlap, and link together, frequently adorned with arrows, curves, and various extensions.

Figure 4–2b • (right) *Stencil* artists use precut stencils to produce uniform and exact letter shapes. Artists craft their chosen letters in a stencil, position it on the intended surface, and spray paint across it.

Figure 4–2c • (left) *Bubble letters* appear as puffy, balloon-like characters, typically outlined and rendered with a three-dimensional effect to enhance their bubble-like look.

Figure 4–2d • (right) *Block letter* graffiti is simple and bold as artists draw heavily from classic typography. They're constructed using straight lines and sharp angles, they form a robust and easily readable style.

In the same way that graffiti art has been criminalized without considering the social context in which the art form was born, we regularly criminalize and subject students to severe disciplinary action for engaging in graffiti art on school property. While some may argue that graffiti art is vandalism and students should not "destroy" school property, instead of focusing on criminalizing their behavior, it's important to consider why students have the urge to engage in graffiti art. Many youth do not have a positive connection or experience a sense of belonging with the school's physical and social space and as a result, engage in graffiti art as an act of self-expression in a space where their authentic forms of expression are regularly policed and criminalized. Graffiti art, as an element of hip-hop culture, serves as a form of creative self-expression and a liberatory practice. Graffiti art exemplifies Black joy by countering dominant narratives and highlighting the expression and multitude of identities of historically marginalized groups. Thus, examining the art itself can reveal vital information about the school context and environment and more importantly student intent. Providing recognition and space for students to express and showcase their creative identities and challenging criminalized views of that expression in schools can look like the following.

Designated Spaces for Expression

Schools could designate areas where students can freely create graffiti art. This provides a sanctioned space for creativity, potentially reducing "illicit graffiti," and gives students a platform to voice their opinions, concerns, and emotions. If your school offers teachers opportunities to display student work, unit outcomes, or images on bulletin boards, consider creating a space where students can provide genuine feedback on sticky notes regarding their understanding, concerns, questions, joys, and/or frustrations around how the unit itself is progressing. Asking students to leave anonymous messages can facilitate a graffiti-like atmosphere where self-expression is welcomed, regardless of whether it's fueled by negativity or anchored in joy. Further, by understanding the messages and emotions behind students' graffiti art, educators can gain insight into prevalent issues among their students. This can serve as a tool for initiating dialogue and addressing concerns, potentially acting as a proactive approach to conflict resolution.

Student Reflective Spaces

Designate quiet, reflective spaces adorned with calming or inspirational art pieces. Work with student leaders to curate these spaces and have students decide when to change up pieces and why. You may choose to offer a reason to change art pieces so that there are new art pieces displayed after a unit ends or before a unit begins as a way of acknowledging change in curriculum. At first, you may need to demonstrate what leadership in this reflective space can look like by taking the lead in making decisions or selecting dates to change the artwork. Modeling decision making, asking for input from students, and sticking to dates will help student leaders establish a routine before they feel more comfortable taking ownership of the space. Stressing that the space is for student use and thus should be student-run supports the idea that the shared space needs their care and curation and that their consent in changes in the community matters. Offer these spaces as havens for students to find respite, meditate, or simply appreciate art.

Environmental Design

Consider how furniture, space layout, and other environmental design elements can create a more inclusive, responsive, and welcoming atmosphere for students. The intention to invite community members to redesign the classroom environment contrasts with the lack of community input in urban planning throughout history. In collaboration with Lincoln Center and Dr. Christopher Emdin, I worked with selected schools to advise communities on how to re-create classrooms to create a sense of belonging post pandemic. A common request from students was whiteboard/dry-erase tables, walls, and floors. Why? Students wanted to be able to write and create on every possible surface. This simple but effective change allowed space for ownership and creativity.

Student Art Galleries

Schools can offer spaces where students can showcase their original artistic creations that were created during students' personal time or as part of class activities. This allows for peer-to-peer education, where students can share and explain their creations to classmates. Just as art galleries curate exhibits, teachers can support students in curating galleries related to specific themes regarding original art pieces. Students can also engage in a process of organizing select pieces to have displayed in a local library or community space as a special exhibition. Other examples of student art galleries include students taking on the role of museum curators and selecting researched artifacts from a specific time period to depict or illustrate understanding or new meaning regarding a given lens in history.

GRAFFITI ART AS CULTURE IN EDUCATION

Graffiti art, during its conception, was villainized and deemed as vandalism. Artists were prosecuted and incarcerated for their approach to artistic and identity expression, which was not yet accepted by mainstream society. Yet, decades later, graffiti art is a widely accepted art form that is now leveraged by communities and government officials to brand, revitalize, and gentrify communities.

In schools today, students across various educational contexts lack access to quality art education and the integration of art and creative expression in traditional content classes. There has always been much contention about the importance of arts in education, with some believing that the arts are a fundamental element of education and others believing that art is a low priority compared to core content areas. Dewey (2005) argued in 1932 that the incorporation of art in education is a foundational part of the curriculum because it develops creativity and an appreciation of the expression of self and others. Conversely, since the introduction of the federal No Child Left Behind Act (NCLB), the arts have often taken a backseat in educational curricula to "core" content areas/subjects, which are measured in high-stakes testing. School districts have increased instructional time for reading, language arts, and math, while arts education instructional time has decreased substantially. In schools populated by low-income students and students of color, there are more disparities as an even greater amount of time has been devoted to test-taking strategies with little to no arts incorporated into education (McNeil and Valenzuela 2001; Heilig, Cole, and Aguilar 2010). This is particularly problematic because lack of art programs strip students of the opportunities that art provides—including an alternative means to view reality and an opportunity to expand perceptions of the world.

Moreover, art is a universal language through which individuals across generations and backgrounds have been able to capture the essence of life and the meaning of human experience. When we consider art in education, it is often confined only to its visual aspects, such as painting, coloring, and or drawing. However, this narrow view limits the possibilities for integrating the arts into teaching. When considering hip-hop as a framework for teaching and learning, we must expand our definition of art to include an artistic worldview—a holistic perspective that challenges and interprets the world (Emdin 2023). Art encourages questioning and interpretation, fostering a critical outlook on all phenomena. This broader view of art opens doors to creativity and self-expression beyond traditional art forms. Moreover, art is deeply intertwined with culture which, in turn, shapes art—similar to how hip-hop culture and graffiti art are connected. Recognizing this symbiotic relationship is essential in education. Incorporating cultural elements into the classroom and across the school community can enhance learning experiences. Students' cultural backgrounds and identities can become valuable resources for teaching all subjects. Art provides a means to connect students with their own cultural heritage, fostering a sense of pride and relevance in their education.

LEVERAGING ART IN THE CLASSROOM: A SOCIAL CONSTRUCTIVIST APPROACH

When considering how to incorporate art to support student learning and understanding, educators must understand that all people, including students, construct knowledge in unique ways. Vygostsky's social constructivism learning theory (Vygostsky and Cole 2018) posits that social interactions, cultural influences, and historical context have a huge impact on how we construct knowledge and make sense of the world around us. It is possible for educators to have positive relationships with students and still not have an authentic understanding of students' realities and experiences. Applying a social constructivist approach by incorporating art in classroom activities can allow students to make meaning of content by leveraging their culture, social interactions, and historical context to create a visual or digital artifact that encompasses the whole student and their culture and background experiences.

For example, in a seventh-grade science classroom where students are learning about the various layers of the earth's atmosphere, Mrs. Chapman tasked her students to draw a visual representation that demonstrates their understanding of the different layers of the earth's atmosphere. To add a critical component to this art activity, students also learned about natural versus anthropogenic pollutants that pose a threat to the atmosphere and were challenged to include its impact in the illustration. In this activity, students distinguished the various layers of the earth's atmosphere, including each layer's distance from the earth, and created a legend that highlights specific attributes of the earth's atmosphere such as satellites, meteors, ozone layer, and so on. Through this activity, students were able to bring the concept of the earth's atmosphere to life. Students included carbon emissions in their visual representations of the atmosphere and created illustrations that convey how carbon emissions pollutants harm the earth's atmosphere. This art activity allows students to make connections between their understanding of the concept of the earth's atmosphere and how they conceptualized the various attributes as well as challenges based on their cultures, social interactions, and historical context—social constructivism. Teachers can also ask students to write narratives that describe their illustration and explain their selected challenge(s) that threaten the earth's atmosphere in detail. Tobias' example (shown in Figure 4–3) demonstrates his understanding of the content and supports the educator in understanding and interpreting the illustration.

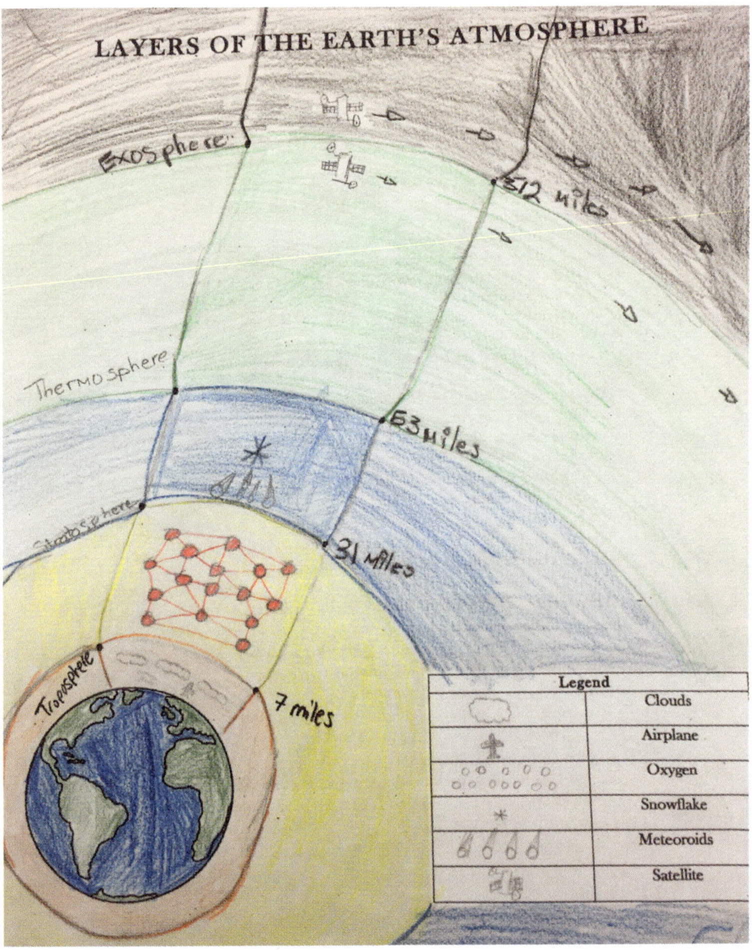

Figure 4–3 • Tobias' student work highlighting layers of the earth's atmosphere

When incorporating activities that emphasize art, educators should also encourage students to interrogate concepts through a critical lens to support students in using art as a tool for critical thinking and interpretation. Through students' artistic and critical interpretations of content learned during instruction, teachers gain insight into students' cultures by understanding how students draw connections to content. The following are a few ways educators can build opportunities to gain authentic and valuable insight into their students' ways of thinking, tap into their various perspectives and points of view, and discover ways in which students may be processing information.

Encourage Critical Thinking Through Art

Teachers can use art activities as a tool for critical thinking and interpretation. Students can create works of art that highlight and demonstrate their understanding of concepts and content, as in the example with representations of the earth's atmosphere. Students can also write narratives, which I like to call "artists statements," that explain their art and the connections to the content/concepts that they are interrogating. Additionally, students can analyze, interpret, and critique their peers' works based on how well and creatively the artistic expression answers the task prompt. Teachers should encourage students to ask questions, identify underlying themes, and explore the significance of artistic expressions in various contexts.

Critical Reflections and Discussions of Works of Art

Teachers have to create a classroom environment where students can openly and safely discuss the cultural and societal themes they encounter through art as it relates to their content. Images can serve as differentiated texts and resources for students to interact with throughout a unit of study. When incorporating visuals, teachers can invite students to interact with visual texts as soon as a lesson has begun by simply asking what they see and what it may mean as it relates to larger concepts such as identity, social justice, and cultural diversity. In this low-stakes activity, an educator creates an opportunity for critical reflection and collaborative sharing of findings without sacrificing too much class time by providing directions on what to do. Teachers can use discussion protocols to facilitate critical conversations to ensure that all students' voices and perspectives are heard (Figure 4–4). Protocols provide timed structure and give students opportunities to both share and listen to varying perspectives. For example, provide each student within a group a different image to observe independently. To do this, place images on the table facing down and ask students to each select one image. Alternatively, you can place the images inside an envelope and ask students to pick a random image to study. After students have selected or been assigned an image, give students a prompt such as "What stands out to you in this image?" or "Do you agree with the image's message?" or "Observing this image, what connection to our current unit of study can you determine?" If the unit is just beginning, teachers can prompt students to predict what the unit may be about. After students have observed the image independently, instruct students to make notes of their observations on paper before taking turns sharing their observations verbally with their group. Lastly, to provide students with an opportunity to engage in critical conversations, give students an opportunity to negotiate meaning with their group by prompting them to bring their findings together. Prompts can include developing a working definition of a concept they will learn about or are confused about. Alternatively, students can work together to decide what these images are trying to communicate as a collective or what competing ideas they are presenting and what they may imply or reveal about a concept of study.

Visual Thinking Strategy	Circle of Viewpoints	Critique and Feedback Sessions
Visual Thinking Strategy is a facilitated discussion model where students are asked open-ended questions about an artwork.	This protocol encourages students to explore multiple perspectives on artwork.	This protocol encourages students to analyze and give constructive feedback on artwork.
Process: 1. Show an image of the artwork to the class. 2. Ask, "What's going on in this picture?" or "What do you see?" 3. Follow up with, "What do you see that makes you say that?" 4. Encourage students to elaborate on their peers' observations, asking, "What more can we find?" 5. The teacher paraphrases responses and points to the parts of the artwork discussed to validate students' observations.	**Process:** Present the artwork and ask students to identify different "viewpoints" (e.g., artist, subject, viewer). Students take on a specific viewpoint and discuss the artwork from that perspective. After exploring several viewpoints, students discuss how these different perspectives influence their understanding of the artwork.	**Process:** Select a piece of student-created art or a famous artwork. 1. Use prompts such as "What works well in this piece?" and "What could be improved?" 2. Encourage specific, respectful, and constructive feedback. 3. Discuss how the feedback can lead to a deeper understanding of the art or inform future creations.

Figure 4–4 • Critical Reflections of Art Discussion Protocols

Gain Authentic and Deeper Understanding of Students

Art can be a medium to explore and express cultural identities, inspiring students to connect with their heritage. Encourage students to draw connections to themselves and their cultural backgrounds when engaging in art activities. Teachers can introduce the Visual Album Strategy. In this strategy, ask students to use the concept of designing an album cover to illustrate an important aspect of their identity. This strategy can also be used to invite students to demonstrate their understanding of content. Begin by explaining that album artwork is the first encounter that consumers have with a body of work. It provides opportunities for listeners to experience the music before actually listening and can add a level of artistic complexity to a musical project. One way to get students thinking about their assignment is by showing and analyzing album art that they are familiar with. Ask students who are their favorite artists and what are their favorite songs. The teacher can also share album artwork that reflects their interest. An example of this is J. Cole's album art for *2014 Forest Hills Drive*. This album cover depicts a hopeful and young J. Cole looking up at the sky from the roof of his childhood home. This allows listeners to understand that J. Cole's album may be about coming of age, hope for success in life, or yearning to return to a simple life. Similarly, students can artistically demonstrate something important about their own identity, showcase their understanding of content knowledge, or highlight key perspectives and/values of a character by creating an album artwork piece. Students appreciate when a teacher provides a model or template of the work that's expected. Create album artwork for yourself that shares who you are, including your background, interest, and identities. Other prompts for the Visual Album strategy include:

- Create album artwork for your neighborhood. How do you want the world to view your neighborhood?
- Create an album cover for a character in the text that we have been reading. The album cover should demonstrate the character's traits, perspective, motivation, effects on others, and personal values.
- Create album artwork to share a scientific concept with the general public.
- Create album artwork to share a mathematics concept with the general public.
- Create album artwork for a historical figure. What ideas would they want to share with the world?

Storytelling Through Art

Encourage students to tell stories through their art. Whether it's visual storytelling, spoken word poetry, or music, storytelling is a powerful way to connect with culture and convey important messages about the world. Through this project, students explore the art of graffiti as a medium to express their personal and communal narratives. Instruct your students to design a graffiti art piece that represents a story about their neighborhood. The graffiti piece should reflect an aspect of their community that is meaningful to them, such as family history, culture, food, memories, or pride. Through this project, students channel their artistic skills to deepen their connection to their community and learn how to convey complex ideas through visual art.

First, students will need to gather materials. They will need:

- Sketchbooks or drawing paper
- Pencils, erasers, and markers
- Large poster paper or canvas for final graffiti piece
- Paints (spray paint optional), brushes, and other art supplies
- Access to a digital platform for those who prefer creating digital graffiti art
- Reference images of graffiti art for inspiration

Begin with a class discussion on the history and cultural significance of graffiti. Show examples of famous graffiti pieces and discuss the messages they convey. Discuss how graffiti has been used to tell stories, express identity, and challenge social norms. Next, have students reflect on their community and choose a theme for their graffiti piece. Themes can include family history, cultural traditions, community pride, memories, or recent changes in the community. Students should write a brief reflection or create a mind map to organize their thoughts on what their graffiti piece will represent. Once they have explored their personal and community narratives, invite students to design their graffiti art piece. Students begin by sketching their graffiti designs in their sketchbooks, focusing on how to visually represent their chosen theme. Encourage creativity in the use of colors, shapes, and symbols that are meaningful to them and their community. Provide feedback and allow students to revise their designs before starting on the final piece. To create the final graffiti art piece, students transfer their designs onto a larger surface (poster paper, canvas, or digital platform). They can use paints, markers, or digital tools to bring their graffiti to life. Emphasize the importance of technique and attention to detail in creating a visually compelling piece. Once students have been given sufficient time to work independently on their graffiti art pieces, lead the class through a whole-group presentation and reflection. Each student will present their graffiti piece to the class. In their presentation, students should explain the story behind their artwork, why they chose specific elements, and what they hope others will understand about their neighborhood through their piece. Allow time for classmates to ask questions and provide positive feedback.

By the end of this activity, students will have explored the cultural significance of graffiti as an art form, reflected on their personal and communal identities, developed their ability to communicate complex narratives through visual art, fostered a sense of pride and appreciation for their neighborhoods and communities, and practiced critical thinking and articulation in explaining the meaning behind their artwork.

Graffiti as Community Art

As we reflect on the historical context and the challenging perceptions surrounding graffiti art, it becomes crucial to acknowledge the constructive influences, creative prowess, innovative spirit, and cultural bonds that have propelled graffiti into the realm of recognized art forms. This evolution has led to its acceptance on a global scale and its integration into mainstream popular culture. Regardless of the type or medium, art holds profound significance within society and culture, serving as a dynamic reflection of human creativity, emotions, values, and thought. Art allows artists to express their authentic selves while transcending language and barriers, connecting individuals across diverse backgrounds through shared experiences and emotions.

Communities across the globe have embraced and supported public art as a way of highlighting the diversity of communities. Community art initiatives have been widely embraced across the United States to foster creativity, cultural expression, social cohesion, and local engagement. For example, The City of Philadelphia's Mural Arts program, launched in 1984, is one of the most extensive and well-known public art initiatives in the world. If you have traveled to the beautiful and quaint city of Philadelphia, you would notice large-scale murals adorned on buildings and sculptures throughout the city (as shown in Figures 4–5a, b, and c). Many murals created through the program depict historical events, cultural traditions, and local heroes.

Graffiti as community art not only educates residents about their own heritage but also fosters a sense of pride in their community's contributions to the city's history. The Mural Arts Program offers creative opportunities for local community members to express themselves while celebrating the diversity within their communities. Residents are involved in the mural-making process by participating in brainstorming sessions, workshops, and discussions on the themes and designs of murals, which allows the community to express themselves through art. Further, local artists are often contracted to design and create the murals—because they are able to capture the nuances of the community's identity and diversity.

In cities around the world, graffiti art is invited to help rebrand neighborhoods that are being revitalized or gentrified as "hip" locations for business owners and home buyers. Cities like Dakar, Senegal; Seoul, South Korea; and Mexico City host graffiti festivals celebrating the impact of graffiti art on local communities. The mural in Figure 4–6 (on p. 112) is located in Grenoble, France.

Across the United States, communities have designed public spaces where graffiti and street artists have opportunities to create and showcase their works of art. These public spaces of graffiti and street art are vibrant and popular as they attract travelers from around the world and contribute to the economic development of communities.

Art is an avenue for self-expression and serves as a reflection of societal values, culture, and thought processes. The community art

Figures 4–5a, b, and c • Murals in Philadelphia are sanctioned by the city.

Figure 4–6 • "Eye to Eye" (2021), Grenoble, France

featured across the city of Philadelphia offers an example of what students and partners can offer back to a community to establish social cohesion and provide opportunities for local engagement with support and facilitation from educators and school leaders.

Community Engagement

Educators can encourage students to engage with their local communities and cultures. Students can explore and interrogate the works of local community artists. Field trips to local museums, art exhibitions, cultural events, or even interactions with local artists can provide students with real-world exposure to diverse cultural expressions.

In collaboration with a media and art teacher, students explored the concept of color theory and its relationship to our emotional and physical well-being through a STEM interdisciplinary project. In my science class, we created hypotheses about whether color impacted our stress levels. Students learned about the scientific method and were tasked with conducting experiments that would assess the impact color had on their heart rate. Students learned about what can cause high-stress levels, the risks associated with living with high stress, and why it is important to reduce stress levels in the body and limit stressors in our communities. For the culminating project, students were required to present their findings and provide solutions for reducing stress to their community and families. Students needed to include strategic use of color in their presentations and provide an example of how color can be used to evoke hormones in the body to help reduce stress at school, at home, or in local and recreational spaces.

To provide students with a real-world example of the strategic use of colors, we took our students to the Color Factory in New York City to explore the concepts of color theory and its relationship to our emotions and physical well-being. The Color Factory has several rooms where students are free to explore and experience exhibits that use color to evoke positive moods. In one room, students sat opposite each other as they participated in a directed activity that encouraged and helped spark creativity while building a connection with a peer. One room, titled "Sing Me High, Sing Me Low, Bring Me Back, Let Me Go," offers an example of collaboration in art and music through featured artists and sisters Lakwena Maciver and Abimaro. This interactive room invites students to exercise their musical talents while simultaneously immersed in a colorful mural. In another room, students answered a series of questions in the form of a flow chart that led them to their very own secret color that revealed something about themselves.

There are many ways of framing a field trip, including supplying students with a worksheet or an activity to complete either during or after the trip to encourage students to make connections between ideas presented on the trip as well as content and skills taught in the classroom. I argue that positioning the activities of a field trip within the demands of a larger project works best. For our project, students were invited to incorporate the use of their secret color in their project in some way or to use any of the colors featured in the museum with a detailed explanation of its use. This framing supported students in grounding their exploration and helped focus them on the larger goals of their project.

Collaborative Projects

Educators can foster collaboration among students from different cultural backgrounds. Encourage them to work together on art projects that celebrate their collective cultural/identity diversity. This promotes inclusivity and a sense of shared cultural appreciation.

To celebrate the diverse cultural backgrounds of my students and promote inclusivity within our classroom, I organized a Collaborative Cultural Mural Project. This activity was designed to encourage my students to work together to create a large mural on butcher paper that would reflect the wide variety of cultures represented in our class. We began the project with an engaging discussion about culture and identity. I invited students to share aspects of their culture that they are proud of or that represent who they are. The discussion set the tone for the project, allowing students to connect with one another on a deeper level. After our discussion, students were divided into small, culturally diverse groups. In these groups, they brainstormed ideas for their section of the mural, focusing on symbols, colors, and images that represented the cultures within their group. It was inspiring to see how thoughtfully students approached this task, carefully planning how their section would connect with others to form a cohesive mural. As the students began working on the mural, they used art materials such as paints, fabric, and mixed media. Throughout the process, they collaborated closely, offering feedback and learning from one another's use of art materials and cultural perspectives. Once the mural was complete, we gathered as a class to reflect on the experience. The students shared the meanings behind their contributions and discussed how the collaborative art project helped them appreciate the diverse cultures of their peers. Finally, we proudly displayed the mural on the wall in our classroom, where it served as a symbol of cultural appreciation. This project not only resulted in a beautiful collaborative piece of art but also fostered a deeper understanding and respect for the cultural identities of my students. It was a reminder of the strength that comes from embracing our differences and working collaboratively.

Community Partner Art Initiatives

Schools can hire community art partners to create public art projects that can be displayed in communal areas, emphasizing themes of unity, diversity, and community. Students should be involved in the decision-making process in regard to what is ultimately created and displayed in communal areas.

Examples of community artists who have participated in community partner art initiatives are Tats Cru Bronx (Graffiti Crew) and Thiiird (Robert Owusu III). School communities working with Tats Cru Bronx have noticed this crew's ability to transform school walls into written messages that transmit joy and inclusion of the community. Schools looking to incorporate art within their space work with Tats Cru Bronx to create and install messages of empowerment in key locations both in the exterior and interior walls of the school building using aerosol spray cans. The school community can collaborate to identify what message and art elements (color, texture, background contexts) best represent the school community.

Thiiird is a multidisciplinary artist with special niche for reworking hip-hop lyrics, symbols, and nostalgic moments into a variety of art mediums, such as neon art. Owusu has worked with school communities to design neon art that sends empowering messages and that reflect the culture to be admired in the school building for years to come (seen in Figures 4–7a, b, and c).

Cultivating educational spaces that reflect the cultures and interests of students will contribute to creating school climates that elicit a sense of belonging for all students, promote diversity in expression and thought, and create a culture both nurtured and curated by youth itself. When students have avenues to express themselves within and outside of the classroom, it fosters creativity, enhances critical thinking, and builds a stronger sense of identity and belonging. The following are examples of how educators can leverage art forms, such as collaborative murals to create welcoming and reflective spaces in schools as a powerful way to celebrate diversity, promote inclusivity, and foster a sense of belonging for all students.

Figure 4–7a, b, and c • Artwork by Thiiird that appears in educational spaces

Collaborative Murals

Educators can invite students to co-create murals with each other or with community artists that represent the diverse backgrounds and identities present within the school. This could include cultural symbols, languages, and imagery that showcase the rich tapestry of the student body. Collaborative murals can work for established school communities looking to freshen up a space or those looking to express, define, and present their identity for the first time.

Educators looking to incorporate art, such as graffiti, into school communities must begin by challenging what is seen as subversive and create, co-imagine, and cultivate spaces for young people to express themselves both in and outside of their classrooms. Communities looking to engage in work with community artists can begin by reflecting on the following questions as starting points:

- What spaces in our school should we consider for community art to exist? What about this location is significant and how will its placement contribute to its impact?
- What issues are currently unaddressed in the school environment? In what ways can community art aim to address these issues?
- In what ways can community art support conflict resolution?
- Are there ways we can build elements for ongoing student expression in community art?
- In what ways will the community art be reflective of students' identities and backgrounds? What information would we need to collect to ensure this?

CONSIDERATIONS FOR UTILIZING GRAFFITI THROUGH HIP-HOP PEDAGOGY

Incorporating art in such an inclusive manner not only educates students about the world's rich diversity but also instills a sense of belonging, understanding, and respect among peers. With art as a bridge, schools can build an environment where every student feels valued and understood. However, for this approach to be effective, teachers and administrators must be open-minded, ensuring that the integration of graffiti art is done in a respectful and structured manner. Educators should involve students in the decision-making process by allowing students to dictate what types of art they'd like to see or participate in creating, ensuring that the art genuinely reflects the desires and backgrounds of the student population. There will be concerns, from potential misuse to discussions about what content is appropriate, and these conversations are imperative to gain authentic insight into students' cultures and how they see and experience the world.

Bringing It Full Circle

Cogenerative dialogues can be a great practice to get student feedback and cogenerate a plan of what works of art are included in the school community and within student tasks in the classroom.

In a world that's rapidly evolving, our approach to education must also evolve. Embracing and integrating forms of expression like graffiti can be a step toward ensuring our educational systems remain relevant, engaging, and truly reflective of the societies we live in.

By embracing a broader definition of art that encompasses various forms of artistic expression and recognizing the interconnectedness of art and culture, educators can provide students with valuable opportunities to connect with their cultural backgrounds, be critical of the world around them, and express themselves creatively. The strategies offered in this chapter can create a rich and inclusive learning environment that promotes cultural appreciation and critical thinking through arts.

5
BARRIERS

Knowledge of Self

The concept of *knowledge of self* in hip-hop, recognized as the fifth element of the culture, is deeply rooted in the teachings and vision of Afrika Bambaataa and the Zulu Nation. Bambaataa envisioned hip-hop as a social movement that could empower and unify marginalized communities. This emphasis on knowledge of self invites participants of hip-hop culture to engage in a deep exploration of their identities, to critically analyze the systems of oppression, and to empower themselves through this awareness. This chapter will delve into the historical significance of knowledge of self within hip-hop, tracing its roots to the values of the African diaspora. We will explore how this concept can be applied in educational settings to support students in developing their identities and critical consciousness, ultimately empowering them to become agents of change in their communities and beyond.

THE HISTORY OF KNOWLEDGE OF SELF

The fifth element of hip-hop, knowledge of self, was coined by hip-hop pioneer Lance Taylor, commonly known as Afrika Bambaataa. Bambaataa's contributions to hip-hop culture are significant and multifaceted and highlight a deep understanding of the cultural, social, and political dimensions of the movement. A DJ, MC, and producer from the South Bronx, New York, he is one of the originators of break-beat DJing and is known for a series of genre-defining electro tracks in the 1980s that influenced the development of hip-hop culture. Bambaataa's contribution to hip-hop emphasizes the importance of knowledge and is one of the lesser-known elements of hip-hop culture. Knowledge of self can be defined as the "Afro-diasporic mix of spiritual and political consciousness designed to empower members of oppressed groups" (Gosa 2015, 57). Bambaataa's vision for hip-hop culture extended beyond artistic expression as he sought to create a social movement that would empower and unite people, particularly those facing oppression and marginalization.

Lance Taylor, a former warlord of the South Bronx Black Spades gang, decided to change his name to Afrika Bambaataa after watching the 1964 film *Zulu*, which highlighted British colonization in West Africa, and traveling to Africa to experience African communities. His trip to Africa and the adoption of an Afro-Islamic name symbolized a newfound commitment to peace, knowledge, and community building. As a result, Bambaataa rechanneled the energies of the Black Spades gang into a global organization called the Zulu Nation, which is dedicated to promoting freedom, justice, equality, peace, unity, and the power of knowledge. It was necessary for Black and immigrant youth to organize in the fight for Black liberation amid the challenges of postindustrial urban decay, gang violence, and ineffective social policies under the Nixon and Reagan administrations. Bambaataa noticed an opportunity to create a unifying cultural movement. He drew inspiration from various sources to use music, dance, and cultural pride as tools to promote positive social change. Bambaataa's approach was not just about creating an artistic movement but also about building a supportive community for youth who were otherwise marginalized and neglected. Bambaataa's strategy involved bringing together the elements of hip-hop culture, which until then had evolved independently. By unifying MCs, DJs, graffiti artists, and breakdancers, he fostered a sense of collective identity and purpose among hip-hop participants.

> **Bringing It Full Circle**
>
> Knowledge of self exemplifies joy as it encourages those who participate in hip-hop to discover, know, and celebrate who they authentically are.

Afrika Bambaataa revolutionized the hip-hop party scene by blending entertainment and social consciousness. He sought to educate attendees of parties by playing a carefully curated selection of music that included pro-Black tracks from artists like James Brown and Earth, Wind & Fire. At his events, Bambaataa would draw the crowd in with popular dance tracks, then seamlessly transition to a more diverse range of music, including electro and Nigerian Afro-beats. This eclectic mix was further enriched by mixing in recorded speeches from influential figures who advocated for Black liberation, like Malcolm X, Martin Luther King Jr., and Louis Farrakhan.

Bambaataa and the Zulu Nation also influenced street fashion by dressing in outfits that represent Egyptian pharaohs, Native Americans, or Afro-futuristic characters as opposed to flashy attire and high brands as a conscious effort to shift the focus from street culture to a more positive and empowering representation of Black identity (Figure 5–1). Further, Bambaataa and the Zulu Nation advocate for an unrestricted exploration of knowledge and recognize that knowledge is truly expansive and unlimited. This philosophy encourages the critical and self-reflective study of

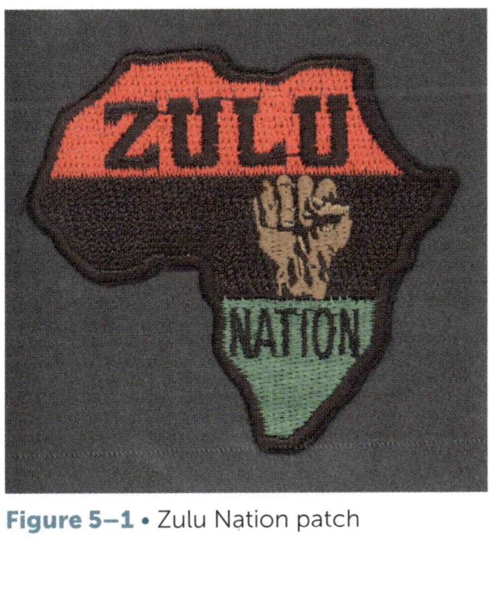

Figure 5–1 • Zulu Nation patch

any subject in the universe as long as it contributes to the overarching goals of peace and unity.

Bambatta and the Zulu Nation advance the practices of the Black radical tradition, which embodies a range of cultural, intellectual, and action-oriented efforts designed to challenge established social, political, economic, and cultural norms rooted in anti-colonial and anti-slavery movements (National Center for Institutional Diversity 2019). Through its holistic and inclusive approach to learning and understanding, which is inherently anti-racist, the Zulu Nation's teachings focus on the commonality of humanity (Gosa 2015). The group's literature illustrates the rejection of white supremacist knowledge found across educational spaces. The Zulu Nation statement of beliefs reads:

> *We believe that through white supremacy, many of the history books which are used to teach around the world in schools, colleges and other places of learning have been distorted, are full of lies and foster hate when teaching about other races in the human family. We believe that all history books that contain falsehoods should be destroyed and that there should be history books based on true facts of what every race has contributed to the civilization of Human Beings. Teach true history, not falsehood, only then can all races, and nationalities respect, like, or maybe love each other for what our people did for the human race as a whole.* (Universal Zulu Nation n.d)

Bambaataa and the Zulu Nation saw a need for hip-hop participants to unlearn revisionist history, the reinterpretation of views on evidence, motivations, and decision-making processes surrounding a historical event, taught in schools that promote the belief that the most significant developments in history are traceable to white Europeans, while the contributions, courageousness, and revolutions of Black, Indigenous, and Latinx groups are downplayed, diminished, or omitted altogether. Schools and curricula contribute to the overall oppression of youth by teaching through curricula that focus predominantly on the perspectives, histories, and contributions of the dominant group, as a result marginalizing and alienating students from other backgrounds. Consider, for example, that at the time of this writing, the new Florida State standards teach students that Black people benefited from slavery because it taught useful skills. Further, curricula that do not encourage critical thinking, debate, and discussion suppress students' ability to think independently, form their own opinions, and challenge systems of oppression. Lack of criticality in schools ultimately promotes conformity and discourages dissent or alternative viewpoints.

Through the promotion of knowledge of self as a core element of hip-hop, Bambaataa and the Zulu Nation have encouraged participants of hip-hop culture to apply criticality to embrace self-empowerment of their cultural backgrounds and identities and to reject white supremacist knowledge and seek the truth about the teachings of history. Through critical thinking, participants of hip-hop develop the skills to question revisionist history, form their own opinions, draw informed conclusions about historical events, and explore possible solutions to challenges faced in their local and global communities. The pursuit of knowledge of self requires the development of (1) identity, which is a complex process in which individuals develop a clear and unique view of themselves and of their personal and social identities, and (2) critical consciousness, which encourages individuals who have been systemically oppressed to learn how to critically analyze their social inequities and engage in action to change them. In this chapter, we will explore how hip-hop culture has historically promoted knowledge of self and how educators can support students in engaging in the pursuit of knowledge of self through identity development and the development of critical consciousness that empowers students and promotes agency.

Bringing It Full Circle

Knowledge of self exemplifies liberation as it encourages individuals to break free from oppressive narratives and societal expectations, allowing them to live authentically and advocate for justice and equality.

HIP-HOP AS A TOOL TO SUPPORT STUDENT IDENTITY DEVELOPMENT

The pursuit of knowledge of self requires the development of one's social and personal identities, which is a complex process in which individuals develop a clear and unique view of themselves and develop an understanding of how others may view them and their personal identity. Identity formation is the mindful process of examining (or re-examining) our own feelings, thoughts, and behaviors (Erikson 1975). This process requires us to explore how we relate to others with whom we may (or may not) share similar commitments. Identity formation is most observable during childhood and adolescence (Becht et al. 2019; Erikson 1975). During adolescence, teens (in particular) embark on a journey of self-discovery, exploring and establishing their identity, which is influenced by many factors, including family dynamics, cultural and societal norms, educational and media experiences, and peer groups. Young people are actively reshaping their identity—as identity is dynamic—by choosing their friends, modifying their beliefs and actions in response to feedback, and continuously reflecting on these experiences to understand themselves better.

Educators can harness the power of hip-hop as a tool to facilitate this exploration of personal identity. Hip-hop often delves into topics such as race, class, culture, self-empowerment, and personal challenges, offering students diverse perspectives to explore and reflect on. Engaging students in discussions about how these topics emerge in hip-hop culture and media platforms can help students learn not only to identify themes of race, class, and gender but also helps create opportunities for students to use this familiar entry point to establish connections between what they think about themselves in relationship to these themes and what they are curious about in the world around them. Figure 5–2a provides a discussion template. Distribute this handout to students and invite them to select a song on their own or provide a song for the whole class to analyze together. You can make learning more engaging by incorporating student perspectives and

Song Analysis for Identity Development

Song:

Artist(s):

1. Song Analysis and Themes:
   - *What themes related to your social or personal identity are presented in the song?*
   - *What key details does the artist use to convey these themes through their lyrics and music?*
2. Exploring a Personal Connection:
   - *Does the song challenge any of your beliefs or perspectives? In what way?*
   - *Can you relate to the artist's experiences or emotions expressed in the song? Share an example from your own life.*
3. Exploring the Cultural and Societal Context
   - *Are there references to specific events, social issues, or cultural trends? How do these references establish the overall message of the song?*
4. Reflection on Identity
   - *How might this song positively or negatively influence someone's understanding of their own identity?*
   - *What aspects of your identity (social or personal) does this song make you reflect on?*
   - *How does the song challenge or connect with your social or personal identity?*
5. Songs Potential Impact
   - *How might listening to this song change someone's view of the world or themselves?*

Figure 5–2a

including students' voices in the planning of the lesson. Conduct a survey among students to create a list of their favorite songs that explore various aspects of identity. As a starting point, Figure 5–2b lists popular hip-hop songs that explore various aspects of personal and social identity. This activity strengthens analysis, which is an essential skill in critical thinking. By analyzing hip-hop songs, students can uncover and dissect themes found in songs that provide perspectives that challenge or support their existing viewpoints and even introduce perspectives never considered before.

Song	Description
"Cobra" by Megan Thee Stallion	The song explores themes of self-empowerment, resilience, and assertiveness, often using metaphorical language to depict strength and dominance, akin to the imagery of a cobra. The track highlights themes of overcoming challenges and asserting one's power, consistent with Megan Thee Stallion's empowering persona in the music industry.
"Tale of Two Citiez" by J. Cole	The song delves into themes of inequality, the struggles of life in underprivileged neighborhoods, and the impact of systemic issues on individuals. J. Cole's delivery is both passionate and reflective, offering a critical look at social issues.
"Alright" by Kendrick Lamar	This song has become an anthem for resilience and hope. It addresses themes of racial injustice and personal struggle, but ultimately delivers a powerful message of hope and perseverance.
"The Story of O.J." by Jay-Z	This song offers a complex look at race and financial literacy, and it's a great conversation starter about racial identity and socioeconomic status.
"Changes" by Tupac Shakur	A classic song that deals with issues of poverty, racism, and social change. Its reflective and critical take on society can prompt deep discussions among students.
"Empire State of Mind" by Jay-Z and Alicia Keys	This song celebrates New York City while also touching on themes of ambition, success, and the challenges of urban life.

Song	Description
"Shades" by Wale	This song addresses colorism within the Black community as Wale shares his experiences with skin tone biases and societal perceptions.
"Self Love" by Dreamville, Ari Lennox, Bas, and Baby Rose	This song focuses on the theme of self-love, and is a great resource for discussions about self-esteem and identity.
"1-800-273-8255" by Logic, featuring Alessia Cara and Khalid	Named after the National Suicide Prevention Lifeline, this song deals with issues of mental health and suicide, making it a potent tool for discussions about mental well-being.
"Wings" by Macklemore & Ryan Lewis	This track discusses consumerism and the quest for identity through material possessions, a relevant topic for young people navigating societal pressures.
"Black" by Dave	This song provides a profound exploration of racial identity, pride, and the experience of being Black, opening up discussions on race and social issues.
"Crown" by Chika	The song delves into themes of self-acceptance, resilience, and the struggles of overcoming mental health challenges, self-doubt, and societal pressures.
"Love Yourz" by J. Cole	This song emphasizes the importance of gratitude and being content with what one has, a vital message in the context of discussions about personal satisfaction and success.
"Can't Hold Us" by Macklemore & Ryan Lewis	Featuring an uplifting message about overcoming challenges and achieving dreams, it's great for discussions about motivation and goal-setting.
"Afeni" by Rapsody, featuring PJ Morton	Paying homage to Tupac's mother, Afeni Shakur, this song delves into themes of motherhood, struggle, and strength, offering a perspective on female empowerment and resilience.

Figure 5–2b • Popular Hip-Hop Songs to Explore Personal and Social Identities

Before engaging students in discussions around identity, it's important for educators to understand how identity is linked to social, political, and economic systems. Students may have never been asked to consider how their identities have either been historically marginalized or provide unearned privileges. Teachers can support students in developing their own identities by having them craft social and personal identity development wheels. This activity provides a framework for you and your students to discuss the intersection of identities and social systems, and how this shapes how we behave in and think about the world around us.

Provide students with the template shown in Figure 5–3. The inner wheel represents the student's social identity: self-categorizations in relation to their group memberships that are often assigned to us or something we are born into (e.g., race, ethnicity, religious affiliation). The outer wheel represents the student's personal identity: a sense of

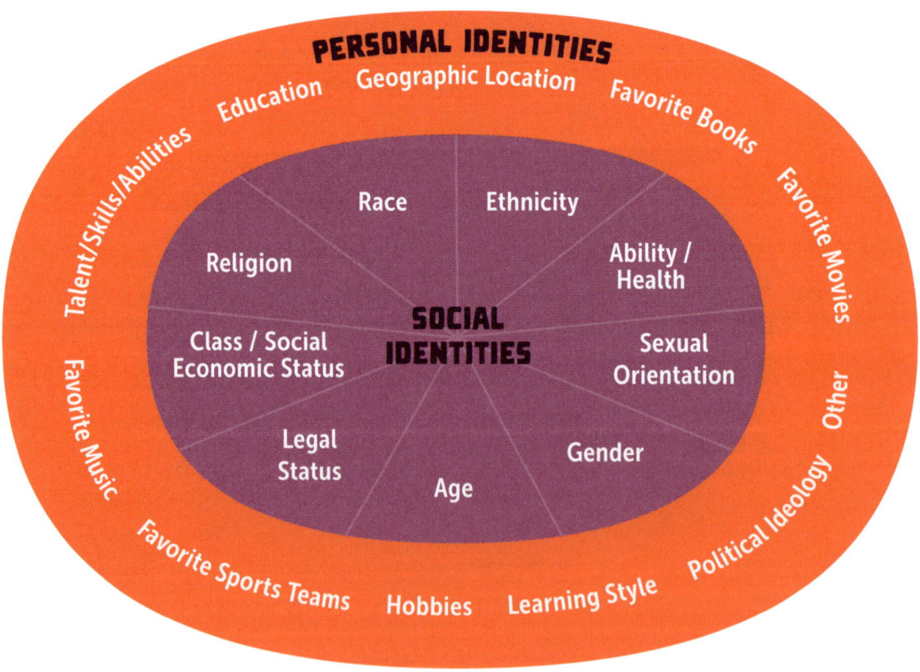

Figure 5–3 • Social and Personal Identity Development Wheel

self that they develop over their life, like their favorite color or favorite hobby. After students personalize the wheel with their own characteristics, students can explore their various identities, how they may intersect, and personal experiences in the world in relation to their identities. First, invite students to reflect on the following questions in a personal journal. Then, with an assigned partner or in a small group of their choice, have students share their responses to two of the questions posed.

- Which aspects of your personal and social identity do you find yourself considering the most?
- Which aspects of your personal and social identity do you reflect on the least?
- Which parts of your personal and social identity would you like to explore further?
- Which elements of your identity most strongly influence your self-image?
- Which elements of your identity do you feel have the most significant impact on how others view you?
- How do your personal and social identities intersect with one another? How does the intersection of identities influence your experiences?

Exploring identity has benefits for all, especially students. Youth who lack a strong sense of identity tend to struggle with self-esteem and confidence and, as a result, may be more likely to engage in risky behaviors or experience mental health challenges (Schwartz et al. 2015). While the benefits of identity exploration and development include:

- **Enhanced Self-Esteem and Confidence:** Understanding their own identities helps students feel more confident in who they are.
- **Improved Mental Health:** A well-developed sense of self can lead to better mental health outcomes including lower levels of anxiety and depression.
- **Better Decision-Making Skills:** A strong sense of identity aids in making decisions that are in line with one's values and interests.

- **Increased Empathy and Understanding:** Developing one's own identity involves exploring and understanding different perspectives, which can increase empathy and understanding.
- **Academic Motivation and Success:** According to Lounsbury et al. (2005) students who have a strong sense of who they are often display higher levels of motivation in their academic work.

THE PRACTICE OF KNOWLEDGE OF SELF IN HIP-HOP

The impact of Afrika Bambaataa and the Universal Zulu Nation on hip-hop culture cannot be overstated. Their emphasis on knowledge and critical consciousness (the ability to recognize and analyze systems of inequality and the commitment to take action against these systems) has deeply influenced the genre, encouraging artists to infuse their work with messages of empowerment of self-identity, resistance, and community solidarity. Bambaataa, along with many hip-hop purists, believe that knowledge of self is a central component of hip-hop culture because hip-hop empowers histrionically marginalized groups to express their unique experiences, cultural identities, and social challenges, giving them a powerful voice to address issues of inequality, injustice, and the realities of their daily lives. Essentially, knowledge of self is central to hip-hop as it encourages participants of hip-hop culture to explore positive identity development, be aware of who they are, be authentic to themselves, and make a positive social–political change for their local and global communities through the development of critical consciousness. This legacy of the Zulu Nation continues to inspire new generations of hip-hop artists and enthusiasts around the world. As educators who are aware of the influence hip-hop culture has on our students, we can leverage the element of knowledge of self to support students in identity development as well as critical consciousness development. Below are examples of how artists have used hip-hop to highlight marginalized groups' realities and experiences while speaking out against sociopolitical issues that negatively impact these groups. These artists and their songs can be used to explore how students' personal and social identities may or may not be shared with the speakers in the songs featured. Additionally, the songs serve as examples of how hip-hop can be leveraged to discuss the intersections between social and personal identities and larger systems.

"The Message" by Grandmaster Flash and the Furious Five was one of the first hip-hop songs to find commercial success and is a prominent example of hip-hop highlighting sociopolitical issues. In 1982, Grandmaster Flash and the Furious Five provided America with vivid imagery of some of the challenges in the Bronx and the social injustices that people from urban communities face on a daily basis, such as police brutality, underresourced schools, and limited access to quality housing. This glimpse into the realities of marginalized groups provides an entry point for the world to understand, empathize with, and even relate to the daily experiences of marginalized groups in the Bronx and other inner cities during the early 1980s and remains relevant to this day. "The Message" allows individuals who share similar experiences in different pockets of the nation to realize that their experiences are not unique but rather familiar and, therefore, promotes communal mobilization for the improvement of social injustices.

"Fight the Power," a song by Public Enemy created for Spike Lee's seminal film *Do the Right Thing* (1989), is another pivotal example of hip-hop artists infusing their work with messages of empowerment, resistance, and community solidarity. In the song, Public Enemy utilizes revolutionary expression to challenge the established social and political structures that contributed to the collective oppression of groups. "Fight the Power" was a call for marginalized groups to advocate against systems of oppression and authorities that abuse their power. Public Enemy highlights the unique challenges for Black people and communities of color, while dismissing the idea of a post-racial society. Ultimately, "Fight the Power" serves as a critical commentary on the social and political issues that affected Blacks and communities of color during the 1980s. Its powerful and direct lyrics, delivered with a tone of confrontation and urgency, highlighted the ongoing struggle against systemic racism and inequality experienced in the United States while emphasizing awareness, self-empowerment, and active resistance against the challenges faced by marginalized communities.

There are numerous examples of hip-hop influencing or reacting to a political movement. In her album *Eve*, Rapsody highlights Black women by addressing common challenges they faced while referencing internal conflicts that reinforce sexism, the emotional toll of the violence inflicted on Black men, and the consequences on Black women of violence committed by Black men. The album *To Pimp a Butterfly* by Kendrick Lamar embodies the essence of American political unrest, capturing the height of debates over police brutality and the rise of the Black Lives Matter movement. The song "Alright" resonated as a beacon of hope and an affirmation of brighter futures, while songs like "The Blacker the Berry" offer a stark portrayal of the continuous struggles faced by Black people in America. In the song "Be Free," a response to the police shooting of Michael Brown, J. Cole highlighted his aspirations for Black people not to experience violence and discrimination by law enforcement. Lil Baby's song "The Bigger Picture" sheds light on the aftershocks that police brutality and racism have on both him and his community following the police murder of George Floyd.

Hip-hop always finds a way to harness the collective feelings and emotions of the Black community. Hip-hop is Black music. Politicians recognize the power and influence that hip-hop has on voters, and hip-hop artists have been campaigning for presidential candidates since 2004. In 2020, the Biden campaign enlisted battle rappers Charlie Clips & DNA to create a political ad to encourage participation from the young Black community. Voting and Black Lives Matter were at the center of that year's BET Hip-Hop Awards, where they hosted a political cipher to remind Black America what is at stake for this year's election.

DEVELOPING STUDENTS' CRITICAL CONSCIOUSNESS THROUGH HIP-HOP AND PEDAGOGY

While hip-hop is a culture that addresses issues of social injustice, it is also a reflection of its participants who exist within the context of the American and global society. As a result, hip-hop can (and often does) promote oppressive ideologies, including but not limited to misogyny, homophobia, and racialized sexism. However, this is not the nature of hip-hop culture; in fact, hip-hop's promotion of oppressive ideologies is a reflection of the perspectives and experiences of some of its participants within the context of the world we live in. Alternatively, hip-hop has always been known to be a contested space where participants are invited to examine, critique, and initiate responses to injustices within and outside of hip-hop culture itself. Thus, while there are aspects of hip-hop that promote oppressive ideologies, there are also aspects that promote social justice. This duality highlights the complexity and diversity of hip-hop as a cultural expression. It is a space where various viewpoints coexist and interact, sometimes in harmony and other times in conflict. While we celebrate the contributions of some of hip-hop's pioneers, we cannot ignore the controversy surrounding Afrika Bambaataa. He has faced multiple allegations of sexual abuse and trafficking. While these accusations cast a shadow over his legacy in the hip-hop community, Bambaataa was removed as leader of the Zulu Nation and the organization has issued a public apology to Bambaataa's alleged victims. The contested nature of hip-hop allows for continual evolution and dialogue as artists and audiences grapple with the various issues reflected in music and culture. Hip-hop often serves as a reflection of and offers responses to societal issues, making it an ideal medium for initiating discussions on topics like racism, socioeconomic disparities, and gender inequality.

By analyzing various forms of media, such as song lyrics, music videos, documentaries, and podcasts that feature hip-hop sensibilities, students can explore and understand various aspects of societal injustice and inequality, which will support them in developing their critical consciousness. Hip-hop sensibilities are the attitudes, styles, and practices that are commonly associated with hip-hop culture, like storytelling, physical expression, fashion, and self-expression, to name a few. Using forms of media that feature hip-hop sensibilities and resonate with students' interests is a culturally responsive approach to supporting students in developing their critical consciousness, the processes by which people come to understand, analyze, and take action against systems of oppression (Freire 1970). The development of critical consciousness in youth has been linked to positive educational outcomes, including increased school motivation and engagement (O'Connor 1997), and may act as a counter to the oppression experienced by students, helping youth overcome feelings of isolation (Watts, Griffith, and Abdul-Adil 1999). Drawing from Paulo Freire's critical pedagogy, critical consciousness in youth—especially those from historically marginalized racial and economic backgrounds—is made up of three interrelated components (Figure 5–4) (Watts, Diemer, and Voight 2011):

1. **CRITICAL REFLECTION** is the ability to recognize and analyze inequality, including interpersonal oppression, such as stereotypes, and systemic issues. Educators support students in practicing critical reflection by helping them develop their social and personal identities, as explored earlier in the chapter. Once students have explored these identities, educators can support students in uncovering how their identities operate within systems of power within our society (for more, see Figure 5–5).
2. **POLITICAL AGENCY** is the belief in one's capacity to create social change. Once students begin to reflect and explore their personal identities, the next step in developing critical consciousness is to get students to understand how their individual identities intersect with one another to create complex experiences of inequity and operate within systems of power. Through exploring intersectional identities, students may find that while they may have some identities that experience historical oppression, they may have others that align with privilege. Through this interrogation of intersectionality (for more, see Figure 5–5), students should be encouraged to consider

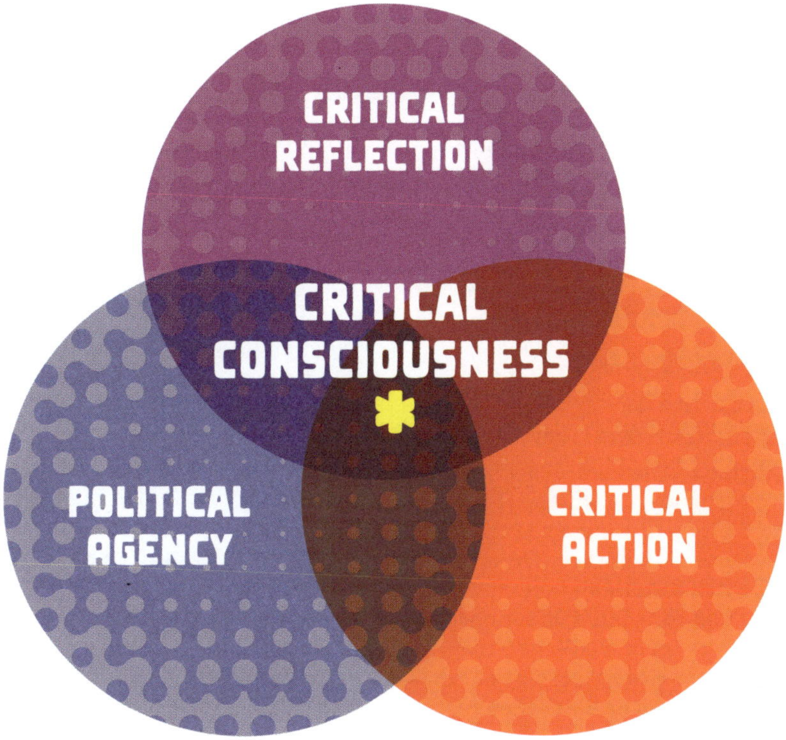

Figure 5–4 • The Three Components of Critical Consciousness

how their various identities may position them to create social change. Once students can recognize their individual power within their positionality and how it can contribute to or support dismantling systems of oppression, they are more equipped to analyze how their social and personal identities intersect within larger systems of power. Explain to students that the existence of a marginalized identity does not nullify a privileged identity. Students can brainstorm examples of times in which they've experienced privilege and power in spaces, what it felt like, and whether they felt or did not feel empowered to make a change. Have a discussion on how everyone, regardless of their identities, can create social change as a global citizen.

[*Example: White Latinx may recognize that they have privilege and power in spaces where dark-skinned Latinx do not. This awareness gives them a desire to act and be conscious of their actions, empowering them to create social change based on their individual power.*]

Intersectionality	Systems of Power
Intersectionality refers to how different forms of discrimination, such as those based on gender, race, ethnicity, sexual orientation, gender identity, disability, and class, converge and create distinct and complex experiences of inequality. **Example of intersectionality:** **Racialized Sexism:** Black women face not only sexism due to their gender but also racism because of their race. These forms of discrimination intersect and compound, creating a unique set of challenges that differ from those faced by either white women or Black men.	Systems of power are the beliefs, practices, and cultural norms on which institutions were built. They are rooted in social constructs like race and gender and rooted in historical events (colonization, slavery, migration, immigration, genocide) and present policies, reinforce white supremacy, patriarchy, and heteronormativity in the U.S. These systems oppress marginalized communities, shaping social norms and experiences, and create structural barriers causing inequities, especially for young women of color. **Examples of systems of power:** racism, sexism, heterosexism, ableism, classism, ageism, and anti-Semitism

Figure 5–5 • Definitions and Examples of Terms

3. **CRITICAL ACTION** involves participating in activities aimed at combating oppressive forces and promoting equality. The last step in developing critical consciousness is participating in activities that promote equality. Once we empower students to engage in critical reflection by exploring their identities and developing political agency, educators must create opportunities for students to engage in critical action. Educators can foster critical action by designing activities and tasks that engage students in demonstrating their understanding of content knowledge and encourage them to advocate for equality. You and your students can identify issues of social injustice that affect local and community issues. This strategy can help your students apply their learning to real-world issues and develop a deeper awareness of social justice.

CRITICAL ACTION IN THE CLASSROOM

Ninth-grade science teacher Ms. Rivera saw firsthand how critical action empowers her students and has ripple effects throughout the community. She began her lesson by telling her students, "We're not just learning science for the sake of it. We're learning to make a difference." On the whiteboard, she had displayed a map of the Bronx, where the school was located and informed her class that they were going to explore health disparities right there in their own community. Ms. Rivera listed a few medial conditions that were disproportionally prevalent in the Bronx, including hypertension, asthma, diabetes, heart disease, and obesity, being sure to emphasize that these are not just statistics; they're realities for many people they know. Ms. Rivera then divided the class into small groups, and assigned each a specific health disparity to research, specifying that they should probe "not just the 'what' but the 'why.' Why are these health issues so prevalent in our community?" Each group was given a worksheet with a list of sources and discussion questions to guide students' research (shown in Figure 5–6).

The excitement in the room was palpable. Students dove into resources, piecing together information on lifestyle, environment, socioeconomic factors, and access to healthcare. One group noted how certain neighborhoods in the Bronx have fewer green spaces, contributing to asthma and heart disease rates. Another discussed the impact of food deserts on diabetes and obesity. As the students worked, Ms. Rivera circled the room, encouraging critical thinking with questions like "How do you think policies and social structures contribute to these health disparities?"

When it was time for the groups to present their findings, Ms. Rivera guided them to identify factors outside of lifestyle and choice that contribute to community health disparities. Students were struck by how economic inequality, lack of affordable healthcare, environmental pollution, and limited access to nutritious food play roles in shaping health outcomes. With the groundwork of critical reflection laid, Ms. Rivera reminded the students of their political agency and shared stories of student-led movements like organizing a health-conscious

Ms. Rivera's Discussion Questions

Questions to Support Research:

» *What do we already know (or think we know) about what the assigned medical condition does to the human body? As you dive into research, what questions do you have about this medical condition?*

» *What type of medical care is necessary to treat this medical condition? Does medication help disrupt or restore homeostasis in the body?*

Discussion Questions:

» *Is this medical condition hereditary, a consequence of specific lifestyle choices, or is it brought on by environmental causes? Is the answer clear cut or a complex one? Explain.*

» *Based on statistical evidence, does this medical condition impact a specific demographic more than others? If so, which populations are most impacted? Based on your research, what could be some reasons for this?*

» *How can socioeconomic factors contribute to the diagnosis and prognosis of this medical condition? Is this type of care easily accessible? What impact does this accessibility or inaccessibility have on a person or family living with this condition?*

» *How do you think policies and social structures contribute to these health disparities?*

» *Do you personally know someone with this medical condition? If so, how does this medical condition impact that person's everyday life?*

» *What did you learn about what happens to the body when it's impacted by this medical condition?*

Figure 5–6

food drive to promote healthy food options for community members and how it can impact the community at large. Students handed out recipes for families and community members to try and invite leaders and organizations to speak on what can be done to support families at the local level. Her mantra for the unit was "Knowledge is power, but it's what we do with that knowledge that counts." Students agreed that they could use their newfound understanding to raise awareness in the community. Raising awareness is a form of critical action. Students designed plans to inform and educate community members about an issue with the intention of influencing their attitudes, behaviors, and beliefs toward addressing inequities. These included creating informative posters to be displayed in local clinics and schools, organizing a health fair in the community center, starting a social media campaign to raise awareness, and even reaching out to local politicians to discuss policy changes. Although some proposed activities were easier to complete than others, none were impossible or out of reach. Ms. Rivera charged her students to work in their groups to bring their critical action ideas to life. She supported her students in this endeavor by adapting her unit's timeline and including additional resources to support students in structuring their ideas for raising awareness.

Through this series of lessons, her students became more informed about the health challenges faced by their community and were empowered to address the inequities they'd explored. They learned that science is not just a subject but a tool for understanding and addressing real-world issues, a bridge between knowledge and societal change. The impact of this lesson will resonate beyond the walls of the classroom into the heart of the Bronx.

Like Ms. Riviera, you can work collaboratively with your students to identify which activities are realistic, considering the capacity of the classroom and school. Some educators and schools may have the capacity to support students in organizing health fairs, while others might create social media campaigns and posters to be displayed at local clinics. The main goal of critical action is to get students to engage with the community to address the inequities they learned and interrogated. Ideally, learning does not stop in the classroom, it extends outside the classroom and into the community.

Planning for critical actions is possible in every content area as shown in Figure 5–7.

Content Area	Examples of Tasks for Social Action
Social Studies	Students can investigate various forms of inequality (such as economic, racial, gender, or educational) within their own community, country, or across the world, using historical and contemporary perspectives.
Math	Students can design an activity that uses algebraic concepts to investigate and understand social inequities. This activity can revolve around income inequality.
Language Arts	Students can explore the theme of inequality in literature, examining how it is portrayed in various texts and how it relates to their own experiences and the world around them.

Figure 5–7 • Critical Action Across the Content Areas

HIP-HOP IS TOO PROBLEMATIC FOR THE CLASSROOM

When I encourage educators to utilize various forms of media that center hip-hop sensibilities, critics often highlight aspects of hip-hop that contribute to perpetuating negative stereotypes or promote inappropriate content. While these concerns are not without merit, it's important to recognize the potential within this challenge to foster a deeper, more critical understanding among students, especially in an educational context.

Hip-hop, like many art forms, reflects the environment and experiences of its creators. The themes of violence, misogyny, and substance abuse that are sometimes present in hip-hop music are often rooted in the real-life experiences and societal challenges faced by artists. While I am not condoning aspects of hip-hop that contribute to oppression and am aware that some facets of hip-hop may feel inappropriate or uncomfortable to use in the classroom, it is important to understand that by engaging students in critical analysis, educators can facilitate a conversation that goes beyond the surface-level interpretation of the lyrics or the image portrayed in music videos. Critical analysis using some of these popular hip-hop elements and sensibilities, like song lyrics for example, can also support students in building awareness of what contributes to their social and personal identities, as well as support in developing their critical consciousness. Additionally, many students are already experiencing and discussing the problematic themes presented in hip-hop culture and it would be beneficial to bring these discussions into the classroom to challenge various perspectives. In dissecting these themes, students can be guided to understand the broader societal context in which this music is produced.

As educators, we want our students to leave our classrooms having learned skills that are valuable to their lives. Knowledge of self allows students to gain awareness of issues that impact those they share a community with. Knowledge of self will enable students to see themselves within the context of the world they live in every day. It allows them to see themselves not as a passive member of their community but as a global participant with personal agency and power to contribute to changes in their lives and the lives of others.

7
NEW YORK

The DJ

The DJ, a foundational role in hip-hop, is responsible for reading the crowd, understanding the mood, and selecting tracks that keep the energy high. This chapter explores the history and evolution of the DJ, from its roots in the early days of hip-hop to its continued influence on the culture today. The art of DJing began with pioneers like DJ Kool Herc, who, in the 1970s, revolutionized the role by introducing innovative techniques that laid the groundwork for breakbeat DJing. Herc's influence sparked a competitive spirit among DJs, leading to the emergence of new styles and techniques that pushed the boundaries of what was possible with turntables. This competition and innovation were crucial to the development of hip-hop as we know it. As we delve into the history of the DJ, we will also explore how the role of the DJ can inspire educators to bring a similar level of creativity, adaptability, and responsiveness to the classroom. Just as DJs use their tools to create an atmosphere that resonates with their audience, teachers can leverage music, technology, and student-centered strategies to foster an engaging and dynamic learning environment. This chapter will guide you in reimagining your role as an educator, drawing parallels between the DJ's craft and the ways you can innovate your teaching practices to connect with and inspire your students.

THE HISTORY OF THE DJ

It all started with the hip-hop DJ. At the center of community gatherings and parties, the DJ's primary role is to select, play, and control the music that keeps an audience entertained and on the dance floor. The parties then served as the perfect context for the other hip-hop elements to emerge. The best DJs have a strong ability to read the crowd, understand the audience, and select music that keeps everyone engaged. This involves understanding your audience and their mood and adjusting the music to keep the energy levels high. At the inception of hip-hop, the DJ was the primary hip-hop element and was deemed even more dominant than the now-popular MC.

DJ Kool Herc is known as one of the forefathers of hip-hop culture because of his innovation in DJing. Herc, an immigrant from Kingston, Jamaica, grew up experiencing dancehall parties with loud and larger-than-life sound systems, which contributed to his interest in DJing. On August 11, 1973, at the party

Bringing It Full Circle

The relationship between the DJ and the MC benefits from their collaboration. This symbiotic relationship requires that the DJ and MC know their own individual contribution to the relationship and recognize each other's strengths and assets. This is an example of hip-hop as love.

- How does this remind you of the symbiotic relationship between the teacher and the student?

he hosted with his sister, Cindy Campbell, DJ Kool Herc introduced the DJ technique called the "merry-go-round." Alternating between two turntables, when the breakbeat ended on one record, he would quickly switch to the beginning of the breakbeat on a second record. This created an uninterrupted flow of music creating a continuous, extended loop that could last up to five minutes or longer. Many people consider that party to be the birth of hip-hop because it marked the beginning of a musical movement in the Bronx, where specific sounds began to gain significance.

As hip-hop started to emerge as a distinct musical culture, other DJs attempted to imitate DJ Kool Herc's style, leading to a competitive atmosphere among them. This rivalry, grounded in an eagerness to innovate, contributed to the evolution of rappers performing over the music. The enthusiastic response of the audience, who eagerly danced to and appreciated this new music, fueled the competitive and vibrant nature of the scene. This combination of elements—the DJs' innovation, the rappers' emergence, and the audience engagement—was pivotal in the early development of hip-hop.

Bringing It Full Circle

The DJ's Connection to Liberation

The DJ element was birthed at a back-to-school party organized for and by the community. Community members took action to create positive outcomes for their members who were returning to school. From preparing the party's music to booking a spot to spreading the word, people came together to celebrate and earn some money to freshen up and welcome the start of a new school year.

Even at its inception, the DJ element inspired individuals to take action and effect positive change for their community. How does this example remind you of hip-hop as liberation?

THE POWER AND POTENTIAL OF EMULATING THE DJ IN THE CLASSROOM

As a DJ, DJ Kool Herc not only looked to incorporate his personality into his playlists but also utilized the turntable as a tool to respond to the crowds' preferences. He is described as wanting to "like any proud DJ . . . stamp his personality onto his playlist. But this was the Bronx. They wanted the breaks (breakbeat). So, like any good DJ, he gave the people what they wanted and dropped some soul and funk bombs. [People] were packing the room. There was a new energy" (Chang 2007, 85). When we consider the DJ's role as one who creates an atmosphere that is responsive to the audience that they are performing for, educators can think about how they can create an atmosphere of liberation, love, and joy in the classroom using music and technology such as digital tools effectively.

The concept of using music to support students' personal and academic development has been extensively researched. The benefits of incorporating music in classrooms and overall school environments include improved performance on simple tasks, supporting students' positive socio-emotional development, and promoting divergent thinking and relaxation (Gonzalez and Aiello 2019). Emotional processes are required for the skills and knowledge taught in school to enter into long-term memory and transfer to real-life situations (Immordino-Yang and Damasio 2007). When a student is anxious, stressed, and emotionally reactive, the amygdala (the structure in your brain that is responsible for processing emotions) responds by blocking the absorption of sensory input (Willis 2008). Under those circumstances, new information cannot enter long-term memory processed in the hippocampus (the part of your brain that transfers short-term memories to long-term storage). Neuroscience research highlights that music with a consistent beat can emotionally affect students. Utilizing functional magnetic resonance imaging (fMRI), Levitin (2006) mapped the brain's response to music. His findings revealed a sequence of activation starting with the auditory cortex, followed by the frontal lobes, and then the limbic system, which releases dopamine. The final activation occurs in the nucleus accumbens, the brain's reward center. These neural pathways suggest that listening to music is inherently linked to mood enhancement (Levitin 2006). Another study reveals that listening to happy music promotes divergent thinking, a mental approach used for generating creative ideas to consider various potential solutions (Ritter and Ferguson 2017). Listening to music not only enhances moods but also allows for learning to be stored in long-term memory for use in new situations to problem-solve.

Despite all the proven benefits, this powerful tool, as with many strategies we know are effective and supportive of student learning outcomes, is often underutilized. Music is rarely incorporated in the classroom. Incorporating music into schools, even in simple forms, can significantly influence students' emotions, motivation, and attitudes. Sharing about musical preferences can be an effective method for teachers to learn more about their students, ultimately supporting cultural responsiveness.

EMULATING THE DJ IN THE CLASSROOM THROUGH STUDENT-CURATED PLAYLISTS

One way that teachers can emulate the DJ is by shaping the vibe of the classroom using music. I encourage teachers to co-curate playlists that are primarily informed by students' taste and choice in music. You can use this activity at the beginning of the school year as you begin to elicit information about who they are and then revisit it when the playlists need updating or during set times of the year to reflect the passage of time, like a change in the semester and/or to embrace a change in season. You can also create themed playlists reflective of larger school events, holidays, or community celebrations and observances.

To start, ask students to identify songs that resonate with them. Invite them to consider music that makes them feel happy, energized, and/or focused. Prompting students to identify songs that resonate with them serves two purposes: (1) it allows students to reflect and become aware of the music that positively impacts their mood and productivity, and (2) it supports you in understanding the various musical tastes and positive emotional triggers of students in the class, deepening your awareness of your students' likes and dislikes, both as individuals and collectively as a class. A template for reflection is provided in Figure 6–1. Remember that you, the teacher, should participate, as well. As a member of the class community, it is important that you share your musical preferences even if they differ from that of your students.

Once everyone has submitted their choices, review the songs for appropriateness and adherence to guidelines, and compile them into playlists organized by emotion. The playlists can then be played

Student-Curated Playlist Reflection Questions

- Which songs make you feel happy?
  - Describe what about this song makes you happy. *Is it the beat, the lyrics, the vibe, or the message? Does it evoke a specific time in your life or memory?*
- Which songs help you concentrate or make you feel focused?
  - Describe how this song helps you concentrate or feel focused. *Is it the beat, the lyrics, the vibe, or the message?*
- Which songs help you concentrate or make you feel energized?
  - Describe what about this song makes you feel energized. *Is it the beat, the lyrics, the vibe, or the message?*

Figure 6–1

throughout the day as background music while students are working either independently or collaboratively in groups. For example, you might play the "Focus" playlist during times requiring concentration and later play the "Happy" playlist during group collaboration activities. Have a student volunteer as the class DJ to organize the playlist for the class. This role can be alternated each time the community decides to update the playlist. Be sure to rotate playlists to maintain variety and continued student interest.

> **List additional emotions you'd like students to identify songs for. Examples include:**
>
> - **songs that evoke a memory**
> - **music that brings you to a specific place**
> - **music that reminds you of a time you felt empowered**

Using music selected by students helps create a culturally responsive atmosphere that is inclusive of student voice and that supports socio-emotional development. It invites students to become aware of how their musical preferences can be leveraged to support their academic and personal goals. It gives students a sense of ownership and control over their learning environment, which can increase their engagement and motivation in the class. When appropriate, you can further support student leaders to take ownership by allowing them to be responsible for updating the playlists and managing the app or device used to play the music. This activity also supports you in building stronger connections with your students by showing an interest in their preferences. Listening to students' musical selections also provides an opportunity for cultural exchange and appreciation, as students may share music from various genres and backgrounds. It's a simple yet effective way to bring the enriching influences of music into the educational experience, fostering a sense of community and shared enjoyment among students.

You may find that you struggle with incorporating music that is divergent from your own musical preferences. You may also struggle with incorporating music that students love and appreciate, but that features inappropriate content or language. I recommend trying your best to find common ground with students. Shutting students down without discussion or student input can prevent future opportunities for sharing preferences and perspectives while finding common ground can build toward an openness to share and contribute. This can look like playing the instrumental or the "clean" version of a song. You can also consider incorporating Lo-Fi music. Lo-Fi music is known for its relaxed and mellow sound. It is a popular option as a background soundtrack for studying, working, or relaxing because its soothing qualities aid concentration and stress reduction. Be mindful to incorporate ways to circle back to music deemed inappropriate in reflection, discussion, or analysis activities.

THE DJ AND THE INNOVATION OF THE TURNTABLES

The birth of hip-hop ushered in a new breed of DJs whose skills evolved from solely using turntables to play music to using turntables as a tool to create new sounds, rhythms, and music, and who, as a result, were called *turntablist*. Turntablist pioneers Kool Herc, Afrika Bambaataa, and Grandmaster Flash are celebrated as the founding fathers of turntablism. They experimented with various materials, technical equipment, and strategies as well as mastered techniques that allowed them to leverage the turntable as a tool to create original compositions.

DJs became competitive in their quest to innovate various techniques and technologies that allowed them to create new sounds and rhythms that their audiences would respond positively to. Grand Wizard Theodore discovered the technique of "scratching," which involves physically moving the vinyl record back and forth on a turntable, creating a scratching sound that the DJ can use to create a variety of percussive sounds and rhythmic sequences. Grand Wizard Theodore's partner, Grandmaster Flash, streamlined the scratching technique by marking vinyl records with crayons to identify breakbeats. This allowed him to switch between records much faster and devote more time to showmanship while DJing, another aspect that separated him from other DJs. Grandmaster Flash, who identifies as a scientist, attended a vocational high school where his interest in electronics was piqued. This interest in electronics and technology encouraged him to experiment with various materials and audio equipment that supported his goals of executing the best DJ techniques that would excite an audience. Grandmaster Flash is credited with several key enhancements to turntable technology, including the introduction of the slip mat. He innovated by replacing the standard rubber mat on his turntable with a custom-made felt pad, which allowed for much smoother manipulation of records and significantly reduced friction and drag. As a result, it enabled him to perform quicker, more dynamic scratching, significantly advancing the techniques and possibilities of turntablism.

Technological advancements dramatically transformed the DJ's role. No longer just record players, they became composers of new music and were pivotal in the creation of new art forms and roles in hip-hop culture, such as hip-hop producers. The best DJs use technology creatively to improve and innovate their craft. New music production software may appear to simplify the art of DJing, but these advances in technology offer new opportunities for experimentation, which, in turn, have led to DJs and producers creating new sounds and styles. As an educator, you can draw inspiration from the evolution of DJs to revolutionize your teaching and pedagogy. Just as DJs transitioned from simply playing records to using turntables as creative tools for composing original music, you can leverage technological tools to transform and enhance your teaching methods, creating engaging and dynamic learning spaces for all your students.

REIMAGINING THE TEACHER AS DJ AND STUDENT AS PRODUCER

In recent years, the use of technology in classrooms has evolved dramatically, reflecting broader technological advancements and the changing educational needs of students. The remote learning during the COVID-19 pandemic forced schools to pivot to virtual instruction and, as a result, personal laptops and tablets were placed into the hands and homes of many students. While many schools across the nation have access to numerous technological tools and learning management systems (e.g., Google Classroom) intended to support students' academic achievement, they do not bring about the intended effects on student academic achievement because technological tools are often mismanaged, underutilized, or utilized ineffectively. Furthermore, the reliance on technology can sometimes overshadow fundamental teaching and learning practices. The assumption that technology alone can improve academic outcomes ignores the importance of pedagogy, curriculum design, and the role of the teacher as a facilitator of learning. Finally, the effectiveness of technology in education often depends on its alignment with educational objectives and the specific needs of students. If technology is used as a tool just for the sake of using it rather than being integrated thoughtfully into the curriculum with clear objectives, its impact on student achievement will be limited.

Just as DJs developed innovative uses of turntables, consider ways that you can leverage various digital tools to support students in demonstrating their understanding of content. You can imagine yourself as a DJ, designing engaging performance tasks that invite students to use modern digital tools to produce new meaning of their learning. Currently, few teachers know and utilize technology beyond simply encouraging students to use it. I would like to see a shift toward educators maximizing the full potential of digital tools by using them with purpose and strategic intent. The goal of this chapter is to support you in transforming the way you use (and perhaps view) digital tools to create innovative and engaging performance tasks that increase student engagement.

Think of yourself as an engineer of new strategies to increase engagement, inviting students to draw connections between content and real-world applications, and supporting students in developing digital media skills. This is the spirit of the DJ: to focus on the capacity to engineer and innovate. Through assignments that allow your students to use digital tools (podcasts, social media campaigns, public service announcements, zines, infographics, and so forth), your students can showcase their understanding of content to address real-world issues.

One such assignment is the digital performance task, which Mr. Myles assigned to his ninth-grade English Language Arts class. His goal was for his students to use evidence to identify the central idea of a text. The assignment encourages students to leverage digital tools to create an infographic, a visual representation of information. The students were asked to select a text they've read and use the infographic to identify the main idea along with relevant evidence that supports their reasoning. Figure 6–2 shows the additional considerations he highlighted for them. An infographic encourages students to simplify complex information by breaking down the larger concept into a digestible visual formats. Note that digital performance tasks can be used

Things to consider

- **Clarity and Focus:** The infographic should have a clear message or focus. Students should decide on the key points they want to convey and ensure that all elements of the infographic contribute to this message.
- **Data Visualization:** Effectively use charts, graphs, and other visualization tools to present data. This makes complex data more accessible and understandable to the audience.
- **Simplicity and Organization:** Avoid cluttering the infographic with too much information. Use space wisely to create a well-organized layout that guides the viewer through the content logically.
- **Visual Appeal:** Use an attractive color scheme and high-quality graphics. The visuals should complement the information, making it more engaging and easier to understand.
- **Balance of Elements:** Maintain a balance between text, images, and white space. Too much of any one element can overwhelm or bore the audience.
- **Audience Consideration:** Tailor the infographic to the Bronx community. Consider ways you can garner the attention of fellow Bronxites.

Figure 6–2 • Additional Considerations for Mr. Myles' ELA Infographic Assignment

to establish interdisciplinary connections. For example, a digital media arts teacher may team up with the ELA teacher to support students in understanding how using designing elements in a balanced way will support the information displayed.

Through this task, students are able to leverage the digital tools to create more engaging infographics than they would have been able to create by hand. The difference between casually asking students to use digital tools and intentionally requiring that students learn how to effectively use them for a specific purpose aligned to their content learning makes a difference in how well students produce new meaning. Asking students to use a digital tool without first modeling how to do so diminishes the potential of the tool. Teachers should be explicit about how to use these tools effectively. This means that educators need to learn how to use these tools first or, at the very least, show an interest in learning about these tools alongside colleagues and students themselves.

For students and educators alike, part of learning how to use these tools responsibly requires gaining digital literacy and media literacy skills (see Figure 6–3). Digital literacy, the skills and abilities to access, analyze, evaluate, create, and communicate using all forms of communication in a responsible manner, and media literacy, the concept of being critical and aware of how media can be used to provide information to influence thought and/or action, are crucial in today's information-rich society. Together, they enable us to navigate and understand the complex world of media. If we don't teach students

Digital Literacy	Media Literacy
Digital literacy is the ability to access, manage, understand, integrate, communicate, evaluate, and create information safely and appropriately through digital technologies.	Media literacy refers to the ability to decode media messages, interrogate the influence of those messages on thoughts, feelings, and behaviors, and create media thoughtfully and responsibly.

Figure 6–3 • Digital and Media Literacy definitions

to use technology effectively, they will not be able to navigate our interconnected world, which is only becoming increasingly dependent on digital tools. If our curriculum does not challenge students to think critically about the media they consume or ask them to reflect on how digital platforms can influence their thoughts about themselves, others, and the world around them, they will be unable to accurately filter the abundance of information—and misinformation—they will encounter. Teaching students how to create and consume digital content is more important than ever. It is our responsibility to prepare students for the evolving digital world, as the need for digital skills becomes increasingly pressing and marketable.

I must acknowledge the challenge of unequal access to technology and the internet, known as the *digital divide*, where students in underresourced areas may not have the same access to technology or high-speed internet as their counterparts in more affluent areas, leading to disparities in the quality of education received (Golden et al. 2023). Even in schools that offer students technological tools, such as laptops or iPads, some students may not have access to the internet at home. Because of this it becomes ever more important to give students access to technology at school. Though teachers may feel uneasy about incorporating technology and digital tools such as social media and music streaming platforms that may initially feel inappropriate in the classroom, it is important to recognize that what we choose to omit from student curriculum and practice has consequences that can impact students' future opportunities.

To support you in integrating tech in your lessons, I have listed some digital tools along with examples of how to do so effectively:

> *A* ***podcast*** *is a digital audio program streamed on the internet, covering various topics. Episodes range from brief segments to lengthy discussions and can feature solo narratives, interviews, or group conversations. Typically, episodes are led by one or more hosts.*
>
> *Students can create podcasts to tell stories or discuss topics, showcasing their ability to structure a cohesive narrative and include textual evidence to*

support their narrative. Students can select key ideas about a specific subject, conduct research, and present their findings to a targeted audience in a podcast format. They can create podcast episodes that involve interviewing experts. You can also require students to discuss topics with their peers, demonstrating their ability to ask pertinent questions, engage in meaningful dialogue, and synthesize different viewpoints. Students can use podcasts to reflect on their learning experiences, allowing them to articulate their learning journey and insights. They can use podcasts to present and support their opinions or arguments on various topics, showing their critical thinking, reasoning skills, and ability to persuade. Podcasts allow for creative expression, where students can incorporate music, sound effects, and different narrative styles to make their content engaging, showcasing their creativity and digital literacy skills. Students may also want to use additional digital tools to create graphics associated with the podcast itself.

A ***social media campaign*** *is a strategic set of visuals posted on social media platforms like Facebook, Instagram, and Twitter. The campaign is centered around a core theme and consists of multiple coordinated posts designed to engage a targeted audience and raise awareness. The series can employ a mix of media including images, videos, and text.*

Students can develop a campaign around a specific topic to raise awareness. This requires students to research the content's topic thoroughly and present it in a way that uses visuals to convey its message. Students can learn how to persuade and influence their audience through this visual medium. They must understand the art of persuasion, know their topic deeply, make effective arguments, and select compelling content to provide reasoning for their claim. Challenge students to work in teams to create a cohesive social media campaign by asking each student to contribute their own post to the project. Students can learn to collaborate by making decisions about which content to include or exclude. Teamwork brings together diverse skills and perspectives. Asking students to work with peers with varying points of view on the given topic can provide an opportunity to widen their perspectives. Crafting messages for social media can teach students to practice conveying ideas in a concise, effective, and engaging manner. Students can strategize for reaching broader audiences, including those with disabilities, and consider what accessibility elements to add to their posts. This can include adding captions for audio and video and providing image descriptions. By interacting with real-world platforms, students see the practical applications of their learning and can grow to understand how the content they are learning about directly impacts today's society. Prior to students creating their own social media campaigns, students can be invited to examine real-life examples of social media campaigns and their impact on the targeted audience. Students can explore the effectiveness based on engagement metrics and learn how to implement these strategies for their own campaigns.

*A **Public Service Announcement** (PSA) video is a short informational clip designed to educate the public about an important issue, often with the aim of changing public attitudes or behaviors. Typically concise, these videos convey their message in a clear, direct manner, often using compelling narratives, textual evidence or statistics, striking visuals, and emotional appeals to resonate with viewers. PSAs are typically* used to inform and educate the public on important issues or updates.

Students can create videos on topics related to their curriculum, demonstrating their understanding of the subject matter and stating its societal importance. Students can explore examples of real PSAs and determine their implications. For example, students can review PSAs about COVID-19 vaccines and analyze their importance in the scientific world and their overall effectiveness and impact on the target audiences. PSAs often aim to persuade the audience to take action or change their behavior. Creating a PSA requires students to think about how to effectively use video production skills to persuade their audience, which involves understanding the subject deeply and making decisions about what persuasive information should be presented to its audience. Recording a PSA often involves verbal narration, encouraging students to enhance their public speaking and presentation skills. As with social media campaigns, students can consider how their PSAs can be more inclusive of groups requiring accessibility features. PSA projects can require teamwork, teaching students how to collaborate, delegate tasks, and work effectively in a group. For example, students can divide tasks such as finding visuals or footage to visually express their arguments, selecting key pieces of evidence to include in the narration, selecting music and sounds to include in the video, as well as editing videos for appropriate transitions, pacing, and clarity. A well-made PSA on a relevant topic can have a real-world impact, encouraging civic engagement. Raising awareness about important issues among the student body and community can support students in seeing themselves as change agents. Students can also share these PSAs in the school community for feedback or assess the impact *of their creations on their local communities. Students can determine whether the PSA brought about the change intended or not.*

Digital zines *are self-published works with a small circulation. They showcase a DIY–style publication that can cover a wide array of topics like personal stories and political commentary. Zines, however, home in on a very specific point in any topic, which is then created for a niche audience and is great for creating items with subcultures in mind. These publications range from simple booklets to more intricate designs, blending text, images, and artwork.*

Students can use zines to creatively express their understanding or perspective of a topic. Whether it's through illustrations, collages, or creative writing, zines allow for a diverse range of expressions. Zines are meant to be a creative, hyper-focused, collection of works of art centered on a central idea. For example, students may want to create a zine about earthquakes. However, the zine format will encourage students to say something specific about *earthquakes. To make an effective zine, you can direct students to focus on students who have experienced earthquakes while in their school community. Creating a zine involves condensing information into a concise and engaging format. This process requires students to really understand the content and think critically about how to communicate it effectively. Zines include elements from various subjects, such as text, poetry, images, and design. Students can integrate knowledge from different disciplines and make decisions on how to best organize the zine, showcasing their holistic understanding. Students can collaborate to create a zine, learning to appreciate different perspectives while needing to combine their ideas to complete an effective zine. Zines can be used to explore and comment on real-world issues, encouraging students to engage with current events and societal topics critically. Students can also be invited to learn about how works of art are published.*

An ***infographic*** *is a visual representation of information, data, or knowledge, designed to present complex information quickly and clearly. It combines elements like charts, graphs, images, and minimal text to make data easily understandable at a glance. This requires students to make decisions about what information will be included and which can be omitted.*

Students can be invited to create and display data, present statistical facts and showcase evidence through maps. Illustrating charts, graphs, and maps help students identify and communicate trends, make and illustrate comparisons, and establish and showcase patterns. They can be used to summarize key learning points, illustrate scientific or historical facts, or present timelines. Doing so invites students to distinguish key ideas from irrelevant or less important ones. Invite students to tell personal stories or present narratives in a visually compelling way that focuses on the emotional impact on its audience. Infographics are effective tools for raising awareness about social, environmental, or health issues by presenting facts and figures and specific impacts on a community in a compelling way. Due to their visual nature, infographics are more engaging than plain text. But to create them, students are required to be intentional about decisions made around the aesthetics of the graphic as well as the information selected to grab the audience's attention. Infographics can condense large amounts of information into a concise and appealing format and are useful when asking students to create reports, summaries, or guides.

As you design your own culturally responsive assignments that incorporate digital tools, remember that technology use in the classroom should achieve two key goals. First, it should help students show their understanding of the subject matter explicitly taught. Second, it should encourage students to engage with their community by applying what they've learned to real-world contexts. For students to achieve these two goals, your task should prompt students to apply their knowledge to tackle social justice issues within their local or global community.

Considerations for Educators Leveraging Digital Tools in the Classroom

The following are some things to consider as you plan to leverage digital tools in the classroom:

- **Technology Is a Tool, Not a Solution:** Like a textbook or laptop, its effectiveness depends on how it is used. The core of education still lies in culturally responsive teaching practices, with digital tools serving as supports to enhance these practices.
- **Align Digital Tools with Educational Goals:** Teachers should first define their educational objectives before considering how technology can serve as a support to these goals. Digital tools should not drive the curriculum. Rather, they should be used as a means to achieve preestablished educational outcomes.
- **Consider Equitable and Inclusive Use:** Address the need for equitable access to technology for all students. Educators should be mindful of the digital divide and ensure that the use of technology does not exclude or disadvantage any group of students.
- **Always Evaluate and Reflect:** Educators should regularly assess whether the use of digital tools is having a positive impact on student engagement and achievement and make adjustments as needed.
- **Consider Ethical Implications and Digital Citizenship:** Remember that you are modeling the ethics of digital communication, including respecting privacy, considering the

diversity of audiences, and understanding the permanence and spread of digital content. A social media campaign series as a pedagogical tool not only demonstrates understanding of academic content but also equips students with vital skills such as digital literacy, communication, and critical thinking. It's a way of learning that reflects the interactive, interconnected world they engage with daily.

Class Social Media Accounts

To extend the idea of making connections with the real world, and supporting frameworks of cultural responsiveness, you can consider creating class social media accounts, such as on Instagram, to showcase the products of student performance tasks. Using social media to showcase students' digital creations is a modern and effective way to extend the classroom into the broader community. A class' social media accounts can facilitate engagement with local community members, parents, and students from other schools within or outside of the school district. This can foster a sense of community involvement and provide real-world feedback and interaction for students around their digital products. A class social media account can also invite collaboration across grade levels, classes, schools, and fellow educators. Further, showcasing student work on social media platforms offers students an authentic audience. Knowing that their work will be viewed by a wider audience can motivate students to produce higher quality work and think more critically about their content.

A study by Dr. Lauren Serpagli (2017), which explores the impact of social media on learning in a secondary classroom found that the use of Instagram served as an effective supplement to traditional classroom instruction. Ultimately, this research highlights the importance of integrating digital tools in education. While using social media may be uncomfortable for some, educators must increase their understanding of the role that social media plays in the lives of students. Youth culture now has a very strong digital identity. However, this does not mean students do not need support in learning how to use digital tools responsibly. Digital tools like video editing apps and social media platforms are a part of our lives as global and digital citizens. It is imperative to ensure students are given opportunities to use digital tools with the intention of addressing local or global issues in their community.

For students and educators alike, part of learning how to use digital tools responsibly requires developing digital literacy and media literacy skills. Using digital tools effectively can support students in learning about the power of media and its role in influencing behavior and public opinion, which requires critical thinking skills and metacognition about what students are consuming and why. As educators, it is our responsibility to provide students with the skills to become critical thinkers in a global world that runs on digital tools.

7

Breakdancing

Breakdancing is far more than just a dance; it's a creative element of hip-hop that, when conceptualized as an approach to teaching and learning, can potentially transform the classroom. In this chapter, we delve into the origins and evolution of breakdancing within hip-hop culture, exploring how this dynamic art form emerged as a response to social challenges and became a global phenomenon. Beyond its cultural significance, breakdancing offers unique opportunities for educators to engage students in kinesthetic learning, fostering critical thinking, creativity, emotional expression, and physical fitness. By integrating the principles of hip-hop's dance element into educational practices, you can create vibrant, inclusive learning environments that resonate with students' lived experiences and tap into their innate potential for love, joy, and liberation. This chapter sets the stage for exploring how hip-hop's rich traditions can be harnessed to inspire and empower the next generation.

THE HISTORY OF BREAKDANCING

Breakdancing, also known as *breaking*, is an improvisational and athletic street dance style that began during the 1970s. It's recognized as a key component of hip-hop culture, emerging alongside hip-hop DJing and block parties. Breakdancers, often performing complex and acrobatic moves, would showcase their skills during the extended breakbeats in a DJ's set, a period when the music features a rhythmic beat ideal for dancing. This synergy between breakdancers and hip-hop DJs during these moments helped solidify breakdancing as a creative element of hip-hop.

Block parties, hosted by figures like DJ Kool Herc, Afrika Bambaataa, and the hip-hop crew the Ghetto Brothers, were vital in fostering a sense of freedom and celebration among young people in the Bronx. As described by Chang (2007), these block party gatherings became "spaces of possibility" for the youth, uniting them through music, dance, and a sense of togetherness. These events offered a respite from the challenging realities faced by community members. Block parties were transformed into spaces of love, joy, and liberation where participants could enjoy and appreciate community. Significantly, these block parties were also stages for hip-hop breakdancers to showcase their intricate dance skills, engage in dance battles, and entertain the community.

By the late 1970s, breakdance was a full-fledged part of hip-hop culture in New York City, especially in the Bronx and Manhattan and among Black and Puerto Rican youth. Breakdancing grew in popularity as a response to the social factors that urban youth experienced in the late 1960s and during the 1970s in the South Bronx. Instead of fighting, gangs formed breakdancing crews where their best breakers would battle one another on the dance floor. Breakers would dance to the rhythm of the beat played by the neighborhood DJ. Youth at the time saw breaking as an alternative to violence and thrived from the competitive aspect and community notoriety that the best breakers claimed. Breaking became an outlet for youth to resist the oppressive social conditions that existed in the Bronx and encouraged youth to contort their bodies as a radical act of joy and liberation. Breaking was birthed out of a desire for Bronx youth to experience joy as a response to the distress brought about by poor social conditions.

In 1977, a group of breakdancers, including Richard "Crazy Legs" Colón and Kenneth "Ken Swift" Gabbert, formed the Rock Steady Crew. The Rock Steady Crew was known for pushing the boundaries of breakdancing during the 1980s with their groundbreaking and acrobatic dance moves that included head spins (when a break dancer balances on the crown of their head, spinning their body around in continuous, swift rotations), headstands, and handstands. When asked about what influenced the art form of breakdancing, Crazy Legs shared, "Our immediate influence in b-boying was James Brown, point blank" (Chang 2007, 117). James Brown, a funk music legend, paired his singing with a distinguished dance style noted for its high energy, fluidity, and rhythm, often punctuated with dramatic, precise footwork. He is best known for his signature moves like the shuffle, the mashed potato, and his dramatic splits. These are the dance moves that would go on to inspire youth in the Bronx to breakdance. The Rock Steady Crew became one of the most prominent groups in breakdancing, gaining widespread recognition in the 1980s through national media and film appearances. They helped popularize the art form of breakdancing by being the first breakdancing crew to appear in a movie, with their debut in the 1983 film, *Flashdance*. The following year, they were featured in *Beat Street,* a film that not only showcased their dance skills but also offered insights into life in the Bronx, as well as the origins and culture of hip-hop and breakdancing.

The art of breakdancing evolved as dancers continued in the competitive spirit to innovate their moves by incorporating elements from various other movement styles, including gymnastics and the Brazilian martial art capoeira (Dossar 1991; Gogerly 2011). They danced faster,

Bringing It Full Circle

The Rock Steady Crew exemplified love for breakdancing as they were known for continuously raising the standard for breakdancing by creating and popularizing new and more complex breakdancing moves.

developed more complex moves, and improved their form. Breakers emphasized their own individual expressions of joy through the use of energy, movement, creativity, and humor in their routines. Since its inception, breakdancing has gained global popularity and has since been included as a professional sport in the 2018 Youth Olympics in Buenos Aires and made its Olympic Games debut in Paris in 2024.

While breakdancing is no longer practiced as commonly in inner cities and amongst youth, the style of dance greatly influenced contemporary hip-hop dance, which continues to be a pivotal part of hip-hop culture. The intricate, well-thought-out, and skillfully executed dances that hip-hop dancers perform today demonstrate a kinesthetic aspect of hip-hop culture. Contemporary dance forms retain the spirit of innovation and expression that was foundational to breakdancing and highlight its lasting legacy in the broader landscape of hip-hop culture.

HIP-HOP DANCE AS JOY AND LIBERATION

The racial disparities exposed and amplified by the coronavirus pandemic, alongside numerous instances of fatal police violence, ignited widespread demonstrations in 2020 in support of the Black Lives Matter movement. These protests drew people of all generations, races, and ethnic backgrounds who united in their stand against police brutality and systemic racism. Hip-hop, born from a history of struggle and resistance, naturally became the soundtrack of these protests. Just as hip-hop and the element of breakdancing emerged in the Bronx as a creative outlet during societal challenges, Black Lives Matter protesters found a similar sense of community and expression through dance. During these demonstrations, dance was not just a physical activity but a symbolic act of joy and liberation in the face of systemic oppression. Participants engaged with hip-hop music not only as a form of protest but also as a celebration of resilience and unity. Their movements to the rhythms of hip-hop beats became acts of defiance and empowerment, demonstrating the enduring ability of dance to communicate profound messages and foster a sense of solidarity and hope in challenging times.

Another style of hip-hop dance, which was popularized in Los Angeles is *krumping*. Characterized by its expressive, exaggerated, and highly energetic moves, krumping was created as a positive, nonviolent expression of raw emotions like frustration or happiness (Peppler and Kafai 2008). In this way, krumping is similar to breaking, where dance battles serve as a form of nonviolent confrontation and self-expression. Beyond individual expression, krumping, like other hip-hop dance styles, plays a significant role in providing opportunities for participants to find joy through a passion for dance. Krumping is more than a style of dance; it's a way to transfer pent-up feelings into positive movement.

Many critics of hip-hop culture today point to twerking as evidence of the problematic nature of the culture. As with many other aspects of hip-hop culture, twerking is often perceived in mainstream society as inappropriate or overtly sexually provocative. But twerking represents a deeper cultural narrative. Twerking serves as an example of joyous and liberatory expression within hip-hop dance. Characterized by rhythmic hip movements, twerking traces its origins to African dance, specifically the Ivorian mapouka dance. Johnson (2021) asserts that the pleasure Black girls find in hip-hop dance, specifically in twerking, extends beyond sexuality, rather, it encompasses the joy, laughter, and creativity inherent in their creative expressions. Black feminist scholars (Brown 2013; Lindsey 2013; Love 2012) discuss how the sexualization of twerking is a result of white mainstream culture's tendency to label Black physicality as inherently sexual and exotic. This perspective, influenced by white hegemony, overlooks the broader cultural and expressive significance of these dance forms. Twerking is not merely a physical act but a statement of joy and a reappropriation of body and sexuality toward liberation. It is a powerful demonstration of resilience and defiance. Additionally, twerking is a natural body movement. Babies and young children "twerk" all the time as an instinctive response to music.

Dance offers a profound medium for human expression. It allows people, regardless of social status, to create spaces filled with joy. Hip-hop dance creates opportunities for participants to experience joy and offers a stance against the oppression they face. Hip-hop, in its many forms, including krumping and twerking, consequently becomes a dynamic tool for both joy and liberation.

HIP-HOP AND KINESTHETIC LEARNING

In any culture, there is a performance aspect where people communicate through dance. The haka, ceremonial dances of the Māori people from New Zealand, include forms that are done before battle (like war or a sports match) as well as forms performed at celebratory events such as weddings. Many indigenous African tribes have dances that serve many social purposes, such as communicating with their gods to ask for rain (rain dance) before the harvest, to prepare for war, and to welcome a newborn baby into the world. In China, performing the dragon dance during festivals and celebrations is known to drive away evil spirits and usher in good luck and blessings for the community.

Gardner's (1993) theory of multiple intelligences recognizes multiple cognitive abilities in humans. Multiple intelligence theory highlights that people use different types of intelligence to support solving problems and navigating various challenges. Among these cognitive abilities is kinesthetic intelligence, learning through interactions between your body and the environment. Kinesthetic learners like to move around, physically create, and touch things. Kinesthetic learners prefer learning achieved through experience and practice. In other words, the kinesthetic learner has to physically feel or live the experience in order to learn it (Murphy et al. 2004).

There has been a lot of debate in the field of education about the validity and usefulness of learning style theory. While scholars theorize that individuals have distinct learning styles—such as visual, auditory, or kinesthetic—that determine the most effective way they can learn, there is no empirical evidence that supports the effectiveness of learning styles in improving learning outcomes (Pashler 2008). Rather than assuming that students learn most effectively through one learning style, I argue that educators should incorporate all learning styles within their practice because we are all visual, aural, and kinesthetic learners and we all benefit from a mixture of those types of instruction/learning.

Through breakdancing and contemporary hip-hop dance, youth learn and create ways to manipulate their body to experience joy and liberation. A hip-hop educator finds ways to deliver instruction through physical activities, hands-on learning, acting out, and role-playing (Lane 2008). Engaging in kinesthetic learning allows students to embody concepts through the manipulation of both objects and their bodies alike.

Benefits of Kinesthetic Learning

When designing lessons, it's important to recognize that students have different strengths and learning preferences. Our responsibility as teachers is to use a variety of strategies to support students in being successful in the learning process. Designing instruction that supports kinesthetic intelligence creates opportunities for students to engage with the material in ways that align with their strengths and preferences, providing comfort and accessibility at different stages of the learning experience. The following are benefits that all students can reap through kinesthetic learning:

> **Improved Memory and Brain Function**—Engaging in physical activity and movement increases blood flow throughout the body, including to the brain. This increased circulation delivers more oxygen and nutrients to brain cells, which is crucial for optimal brain function. Further, the movement stimulates the release of various neurochemicals, such as endorphins and dopamine, which are known to aid in cognitive functions, including memory. Movement is also linked to increased neuroplasticity, the brain's ability to form new neural connections (Hötting and Röder 2013), which is fundamental to learning (Hammond 2014). Engaging in physical activity and movement while learning can support and improve the memory and brain function of students.
>
> **Increases Focus and Attention**—Learning new material requires a significant amount of executive functioning in terms

of attention and concentration. Schools often follow models of "bell-to-bell instruction," which assumes that students are engaging in high cognitive demand for the entirety of the class period, from the success starter (or do now) to the exit ticket. The challenge with this is that the expectation for learning through every period of the day allows little time for students to take brain breaks. Sustaining attention over long periods of time is challenging. Creating opportunities for students to engage in movement within the classroom can be invigorating, leading to increased focus and attention, which can, in turn, aid in content knowledge acquisition.

Physical Health Benefits—Physical and mental health are interconnected and are key facets of our overall well-being. A healthy body provides a solid foundation for a strong and healthy mind. Physical health directly affects brain health. Adequate nutrition, exercise, and sleep, which are pillars of physical health, play crucial roles in cognitive functions, including memory, attention, and problem-solving. Practicing exercise and engaging in physical activity within school spaces can model the importance of physical and mental health for students, as well as highlight that good physical health is ideal for learning. It is important to note that teachers are not physicians, nutritionists, or other health professionals (unless you also happen to be). It is not your responsibility to diagnose or "treat" health conditions. However, you can support students to develop habits that lead to good health.

Stress Reduction—Students bring stress from their personal lives into the classroom as well as the stress that is created from educational pursuits. Stress activates the body's fight or flight response, which in high-stress situations can be detrimental when prolonged. Regular stress can ultimately impair students' brain function, particularly in areas related to memory and focus (Córdova et al. 2023). While students experience stress on a daily basis, it is important to support them in developing stress management skills through metacognition. Instead of solely focusing on reducing stress for students, we should focus on supporting students in building resilience by guiding them through stress-recovery cycles and teaching them to recognize and manage stress independently. You can discuss stress regularly during class or during check-ins with students. You can also encourage students to reflect on their stress levels and recognize the signs of stress in themselves. This can be done through journaling, class discussions, or quick check-ins. By guiding students on how to recognize and address stress regularly, you empower them to develop the awareness and skills needed to manage stress in various contexts. Constant experiences and the lack of proper stress management can lead to the overproduction of stress hormones like cortisol, which can negatively affect brain functioning, including neural growth and synaptic regulation (Yaribeygi et al. 2017).

STRATEGIES TO PROMOTE PHYSICAL MOVEMENT AND LEARNING

Promoting physical movement in the classroom not only supports students' physical health but also enhances cognitive function, engagement, and overall learning. The following are several strategies to integrate physical movement into learning.

Movement Breaks

Classroom movement breaks are a strategic approach to integrate short periods—about 5 minutes—of physical activity into the classroom routine to support student learning. Movement breaks are scheduled as part of a student's overall school day or class period, involve simple calisthenic physical activities or stretching exercises, and are designed to be inclusive and adaptable for all students. The benefits of incorporating these movement breaks are multifaceted. They enhance cognitive functions by reinvigorating the mind, leading to improved concentration and better memory retention, which are essential for effective learning (Braniff 2011). From a physical standpoint, regular physical movement not only boosts fitness levels, strength, and flexibility of students but also encourages the formation of healthy lifestyle habits. Importantly, movement breaks play an essential role in mental well-being by reducing stress and elevating mood (Braniff 2011).

For successful implementation, establish clear guidelines, involve students in the activity selection, and continually seek feedback for adjustments. Students will begin to anticipate movement breaks if you use them consistently. For example, if you teach a 90-minute block, you may want to consider implementing a movement break somewhere around the half-time mark. If you, in collaboration with other grade team teachers, want to incorporate movement breaks into your students' day, you can implement the movement break during the same period consistently (for example, fourth period daily) or in the same class consistently (for example, science class). I encourage you to consider having a student co-teach and lead the movement breaks to empower students to take ownership of the classroom environment and of leading their peers. Figures 7–1 and 7–2 offer some movement break activities to use as starting points, but there are many more.

Calisthenic Exercise	Description	Instructions	Modification
Jumping Jacks	A classic cardio exercise that involves jumping with legs and arms moving in and out.	Students stand with feet together, hands at sides. Jump while raising arms overhead and spreading legs apart. Return to the starting position and repeat. Ensure students have enough space around them.	Step one foot out to the side at a time instead of jumping. Raise arms overhead, then bring them back down. Repeat on the other side.

Calisthenic Exercise	Description	Instructions	Modification
Scissor Kicks	This exercise targets the legs and core, mimicking a scissor motion with the legs.	Students sit on the edge of a chair, leaning slightly back, holding the sides for support. Extend legs out in front, slightly off the ground. Alternate crossing legs over each other like scissors.	Perform the movement while lying on the back, with hands placed under the hips for support.
Jog in Place	Jogging but done in a stationary position is good for light cardio.	Students stand in place and jog, lifting their knees alternately. Keep the pace steady and ensure there's enough room around each student.	March in place instead of jogging, focusing on lifting the knees high.
Mountain Climbers	A full-body workout that simulates climbing.	Students get into a plank position (use a desk or wall for support if needed). Bring one knee towards the chest, then switch to the other knee, moving them in a "running" motion.	Perform the exercise at a slower pace or with hands on a raised surface like a bench or desk.
Invisible Jump Rope	Simulates jump rope movements without the actual rope, focusing on coordination and cardio.	Students stand with their feet slightly apart and pretend to hold a jump rope. Jump with both feet at the same time, mimicking the motion of jumping over a rope. Keep elbows close to the body.	Perform a step-touch movement from side to side while mimicking the arm motion of jumping rope.
Squats	A fundamental exercise that strengthens the lower body and core.	Students stand with feet shoulder-width apart. Bend knees, lowering the body as if sitting in a chair, then stand back up. Keep back straight and knees behind toes.	Use a chair to guide depth—sit down and stand back up.

Figure 7–1 • Movement Break Exercises

Stretch	Instructions
Arm Stretch	Extend one arm across your body. Use your other arm to pull the extended arm gently toward your chest. Hold for a few seconds, then switch arms. This stretch works the shoulders and arms.
Seated Forward Bend	Sit at the edge of your chair with your legs together. Inhale and lift your arms up overhead. As you exhale, bend forward at the hips, lowering your hands toward your ankles or feet. Hold for a few breaths, then sit up. This stretch is great for the spine and hamstrings.
Torso Stretch	Sit up straight in your chair. Place your right hand on the back of the chair and twist your torso to the right, looking over your right shoulder. Hold for a few seconds, then switch to the left side. This stretch is good for the lower back and torso.

Figure 7–2 • Movement Break Stretches

Role-Playing

Role-playing, a form of experiential learning, offers students a dynamic way to learn by acting out roles of assigned characters, positions, components of processes, or any given situation (Russell and Shepherd 2010). This can be done individually, in pairs, or in small groups, depending on the complexity of the scenario. The goal is for students to immerse themselves in real-life scenarios and use their understanding of content knowledge and concepts to make meaning of the assigned scenario. This pushes students to engage deeply with the content, understand different perspectives, and explore their own reactions and feelings in the classroom environment. Role-play is versatile and can be used across various subjects and educational levels, helping students grasp complex or ambiguous concepts through practical, hands-on experience.

There are many benefits of role-play for student learning. Cognitively, it supports students in connecting theory with practice, making learning concepts more concrete. Role-play provides socio-emotional skill-building by encouraging empathy and self-reflection as students step into others' shoes. Finally, role-play offers a rehearsal space for applying best practices in real-life situations. Research has consistently shown that role-play can effectively enhance learning outcomes, making it a valuable tool in modern education (Nestel and Tierney 2007).

When planning a role-play activity, you must have a clear idea of the concepts that you want students to interrogate as well as clearly defined roles that will guide the students in their interactions. Sample role-plays in various content areas are provided in Figure 7–3.

Content Area	Examples of Role-Play
Science	In a science classroom, students can simulate the behavior of particles in different states of matter through their physical movements, guided by changes in "energy" represented by the volume level of a hip-hop song (teachers can use a song from student-curated playlists). Students are told that the four walls of the classroom represent a closed container and that each student represents a particle within the closed container. Students are told that the class is in a solid state of matter. The teacher plays the song at a low volume, indicating very low energy, and as a result, students gather closely together on one side of the room and limit their movements, mimicking the tightly packed particles of a solid in a fixed position. When the teacher increases the volume slightly, indicating a rise in energy, students are told that they are in the liquid state of matter. As a result, students begin to roll along one side of the classroom, representing liquid particles that take the shape of the container. Finally, the teacher shares that the class is now in the gas state of matter and raises the volume of the music. As a result, students energetically move around the classroom at a faster pace, occasionally "bumping" into one another to represent the high-energy, independent movement of particles in a gaseous state. This dynamic role-play is designed to help students visually, aurally, and physically understand the concepts of particle behavior in different states of matter.
Social Studies	In a social studies classroom, students explore the historical contributions of Black feminist activists such as Audre Lorde, Dorothy Height, Ida B. Wells, and Sojourner Truth. Before students engage in role-play, they explore the biographical summaries and key writings and speeches of their historical figure. Students are given modern-day issues and are responsible for acting as their selected historical figure might respond. For example, students can respond to the United States Supreme Court decision to overturn Roe v. Wade through the perspective of their selected historical figure. Students can orally present their response to the class. Students can engage in this activity in small groups or individually.

Continues

Continued from previous page

Content Area	Examples of Role-Play
Social Studies (*continued*)	Through this activity, students deepen their understanding of the diverse perspectives within the Black feminist movement and examine the varied contexts in which these women advocated for justice and equality.
English Language Arts	In an English Language Arts class, students can gain a deeper understanding of a novel or play through an activity called the "Character Council Meeting." Each student is assigned a character from the text and creates a detailed profile, including motivations, conflicts, and relationships. The classroom is set up to resemble a council meeting, with chairs arranged in a circle and an agenda displayed that outlines key topics for discussion. The activity begins with students warming up by introducing themselves in character and briefly discussing their character's perspective with a partner. Once the council meeting starts, students stay in character, discussing major events and decisions from the story, using quotes and interactions that reflect their characters' views and relationships. The teacher or a student moderator guides the discussion, ensuring that all characters have a voice.
Math	In a math classroom, students can be tasked to work in small groups to physically represent and balance algebraic equations. Each student receives a stack of cards featuring numbers, variables, and mathematical symbols (i.e., +, −, ×, ÷, ≥, ≤, ≠). Groups of about 4–5 students must then arrange themselves in an order that correctly forms a valid mathematical equation, such as arranging the cards (for example, "3," "×," "=," "12," and "4" to display "3 × 4 = 12"). In groups, students discuss and negotiate the arrangement to achieve the correct balance. Once students believe they have formed a correct equation, the educator verifies their answer. If incorrect, the teacher can provide a hint without revealing the specific error, and students try again. Upon successful verification, groups receive more challenging sets of cards.

Figure 7–3 • Examples of Role-Play by Content Area

All role-play activities should end with a debrief. Debriefing allows students to reflect on their experiences, synthesize the lessons learned, and integrate them more deeply into their understanding. This process ensures that the educational objectives of the role-play are fully realized, as students get the opportunity to discuss what they did, how they felt, and the implications of their decisions within the simulated scenario. Additionally, incorporating constructive feedback during and after the role-play helps students to immediately understand and rectify any misconceptions or errors, improving their performance and engagement in real-time. Feedback also serves as a guiding tool that helps students refine their strategies and approaches in future scenarios, fostering a learning environment that emphasizes growth and continuous improvement. This combination of debriefing and feedback not only solidifies learning but also makes the educational experience more dynamic and responsive to student needs, ultimately leading to a more thorough and reflective educational process. Questions that you can ask students during these role-playing sessions include:

- What role did you play, and what were the main responsibilities of your character?
- How did you feel during the role-play?
- What were the biggest challenges you faced during the role-play?
- How did the actions of others affect your decisions and actions?
- What did you learn from this role-play about the topic explored?

Card Sorting

Card sorting is a kinesthetic learning strategy that fosters critical thinking by allowing students to physically manipulate and organize cards related to their study topic. Students are given cards that contain data relevant to the subject matter, such as words, numbers, or images. The goal is for students to classify, sequence, or group the cards based on specific criteria to demonstrate an understanding of concepts that align with the learning goals.

Card sorting is effective because it encourages students to be in charge of their own learning process and requires physical engagement. This interaction deepens their understanding and helps anchor the concepts more firmly in their minds. The sorting requires students to apply higher-order thinking skills. Students must analyze the information on each card, synthesize this information to see how the cards relate to each other, and evaluate where each card fits best according to the sorting criteria. This process not only helps in better understanding and retention of the material but also in developing critical thinking skills that are essential across all areas of education. Card sorting also engages students in multiple senses. Students not only engage in kinesthetic touch but also see how information can be sequenced and work collaboratively with peers, integrating visual, verbal, and tactile learning. Working together allows students to discuss and justify their choices, consider different viewpoints, and collaboratively draw conclusions.

This chapter highlights the cultural and educational significance of breakdancing and hip-hop dance. We traced the origins of breakdancing as creative responses to social challenges and their evolution into a global phenomenon, even seen on the world stage of the 2024 Olympic Summer Games in Paris. It highlights how these dance forms serve as powerful tools for personal expression, community building, and resistance against oppression. I advocate for the integration of kinesthetic learning in education as this chapter illustrates. By engaging students in physical movement, educators can tap into the benefits of kinesthetic learning style, improving memory, focus, physical health, and stress management. The strategies outlined—such as movement breaks, role-playing, and card sorting—demonstrate practical ways to integrate physical activity into the learning process, making education more dynamic, inclusive, and responsive to the diverse needs of students.

CONCLUSION

YOU GOT A STORY TO TELL

If you have made it this far, you must be committed to using hip-hop as an approach to teaching in your classroom or educational setting. I appreciate your consideration and commitment to supporting positive academic and social outcomes for young people. In this book, I've discussed the many benefits of hip-hop pedagogy. I often tell educators that if we were to remove hip-hop conceptualization from this framework, hip-hop pedagogy would just be reflective of good teaching practices. It serves as both a culturally responsive way of engaging youth and a way to incorporate multiple modalities within the instruction. However, hip-hop pedagogy *is* a form of teaching derived from hip-hop culture, and because of this, at its core, it's an inclusive approach to teaching that caters to various types of learners and encourages students to engage in content through its hip-hop sensibilities and elements. As it is necessary to give teachers credit for their hard work and dedication, it is necessary to credit the roots of hip-hop pedagogy practices, which are grounded in hip-hop and Black cultures.

I understand that the role of the educator is multifaceted and yet devalued. We serve many roles within a school community. We are teachers, mentors, guidance counselors, extended family members, and so on. We provide guidance on career and college pathways and offer advice on social relationships, academics, and overall emotional well-being. We care for students beyond the classroom walls and form relationships with families and community stakeholders. We even serve as emergency contacts and pseudo-family members. Yet, despite the many roles we serve, even outside of our many responsibilities as educators, the public perception of education and teachers seems negative. We saw the this highlighted during the COVID-19 pandemic when nearly all schools across the nation were forced to transition, practically overnight, to remote learning, many without plans in place. Teachers were expected to know how to transition to teaching students online without students having the digital resources to do so. Due to working from home restrictions, we were expected to further blur the lines between our personal time and work time. We were even expected to protect students from the health risks brought on by the pandemic itself. Even in the midst of the pandemic, politicians and parents demanded that teachers return to school buildings and advocated for schools to remain open even without proper and effective safety protocols in place to protect us and our students. Many teachers faced stress and burnout during this time, and we saw a massive teacher shortage as a result.

However, these negative perceptions are not new. Teachers have long been perceived in a negative light in the media, which contributes to the negative public perception. Movies like *Bad Teacher* and *Mean Girls* depict the teacher as either clueless, unconcerned with their role as an educator, or an inappropriate role model. Media does not depict the realities of a committed teacher and rarely feature the long nights of assessing student work, the amount of time it takes us away from our families when planning over the weekends, or the constant thinking and rethinking or adapting of a lesson or project to fit student needs and school changes. Media does not reflect committed teachers' sacrifice and dedication to our students and to the communities we serve, nor does it reflect the impact politics and policies have on our chosen profession.

As a result of the "anti-woke" movement in education, which broadly opposes concepts and policies related to critical race theory, gender identity, and comprehensive sexual education, among others, our jobs are further politicized. Organizations and politicians in support of the "anti-woke" movement have advocated for laws that limit and even ban books that address issues of diversity, equity, inclusion, and belonging (DEIB) across some states. As a result, across the nation, both in states where DEIB books are banned and even in states where they are not, teachers who consider using teaching approaches, text, and resources that connect to the lives and experiences of historically marginalized students in the classroom are in fear of losing their jobs or being ostracized by colleagues and parents.

In response to the increasing duties and demands, it is very common for educators to experience burnout and low morale. Educator tropes in the media, and the hyper-politicization of the profession are not new and have existed for decades, and further add stress to an already high-stress and demanding profession. Educators need encouragement and support and to be seen in media and society in a way that values the craft. Preservice educators need to see the role properly reflected in the media so their expectations are accurate. Without these supports, educators can be left feeling neglected, powerless, and unable to meet demands.

It's my hope that teachers gain a sense of excitement and connection when leveraging hip-hop pedagogy in their classrooms. When you incorporate hip-hop in your classrooms, despite your innovations and intentions to push love, joy, and liberation further, you may face some criticism because of how society views hip-hop culture and Black youth. I encourage you to direct your school leaders, colleagues, and parents to the plethora of hip-hop education research that exists. You can inspire your community by highlighting hip-hop pedagogy in your practice as an effective approach across a multitude of content areas and grade levels. These changes can and do begin with you.

PROTECTING YOUR MENTAL

This work is hard and may feel isolating at times. To persist in it, you will need to protect your mental well-being. The following strategies were designed with your well-being in mind because you deserve just as much joy, love, and liberation as your students.

Find Your Community

Finding a community of like-minded educators is essential for sustaining and enriching your teaching practice, especially in environments where culturally responsive frameworks may face opposition. It can be challenging to navigate these spaces alone, and while your immediate school environment might not offer the support you need, there are numerous avenues to connect with peers who share your values and educational goals. Look beyond your school to the broader school district or even on a state and national level to find networks of educators committed to similar teaching principles—there's no geographical limit to the community. Social media platforms can be invaluable resources for finding community because you can access diverse groups and social networks where educators discuss their experiences, share resources, and offer support. Platforms like X, formerly Twitter, have networks of educators who engage and champion culturally responsive teaching approaches. Sometimes, it's easy to believe that we are alone in this work, but we are not—we simply have to find our community.

The #HipHopEd Virtual Learning Community

The #HipHopEd virtual community gathers educators, scholars, students, and community members across social media platforms to explore the intersections of hip-hop culture and education. Established on Twitter in 2010, this virtual professional learning community has grown to include over 18,000 participants across all social media platforms sharing resources, discussing challenges, and developing strategies to integrate hip-hop into educational settings. Follow #HipHopEd on all social media platforms to interact and engage with the HipHopEd virtual community.

Small Wins Jar

The "Small Wins Jar" is a mental health strategy aimed at cultivating gratitude and recognizing daily achievements. Educators can engage in this practice by obtaining a jar, which they can personalize to their liking, along with a collection of small pieces of paper or note cards.

As you encounter positive moments throughout your day—be it a breakthrough with a student, a well-received lesson, or even a small professional accomplishment—jot it down on paper. The note is then folded and placed inside the jar, serving as tangible reminders of your successes.

This practice not only allows educators to reflect on positive experiences as they happen but also provides a repository of uplifting memories to draw from during challenging times. You can open your jar at any time to revisit your small wins and to be reminded of the positive impact of your work and the progress that you make daily, which can be especially encouraging during periods of stress or burnout. Continuously adding to the jar encourages a habitual focus on the positive, helping to build resilience and sustain a high level of professional satisfaction and well-being.

Self-Compassion

Engaging in self-compassion is a powerful way for educators to support their mental health and cope with the daily pressures and challenges of the profession. Self-compassion involves treating yourself with kindness, recognizing your shared humanity, and being mindful of the language you use when confronting challenging thoughts or feelings.

The following are some ways teachers can cultivate self-compassion to enhance their well-being. I encourage you to try them all:

- **Practice Mindful Awareness:** Acknowledge your feelings without judgment. This could be stress, frustration, or disappointment. Recognizing and naming these emotions is the first step in dealing with them compassionately.
- **Positive Self-Talk:** Notice when you are being self-critical and replace critical thoughts with kinder, gentler ones. For example, replace "I'm a bad teacher" with "I'm doing my best with what I have, and I'm learning from my experiences."
- **Regular Self-Reflection:** Engage in regular self-reflection through journaling or meditation, focusing on what you've learned and how you've grown rather than what didn't go as

planned. Consider how and who you can reach out to for constructive feedback as an opportunity for growth in your practice.

- **Forgiveness and Acceptance:** Cultivate an attitude of forgiveness toward yourself, your students, and the systems in which you operate. This involves recognizing that we are not perfect, students are not perfect, and the institution of school is also imperfect. Accepting this reality and forgiving yourself and your students for mistakes is important for self-compassion.

Self-Care

Practicing self-care is essential for teachers to maintain their well-being, reduce stress, and sustain our effectiveness in the classroom. We are well aware that the demands of teaching can be overwhelming and filled with emotional labor and the constant pressure to meet the needs of diverse learners. Without intentional self-care, we are at risk of burnout. By prioritizing our own mental, emotional, and physical health, we can recharge our energy and maintain our passion for teaching. I always say that a well-cared-for teacher is better equipped to create a positive, nurturing classroom environment, think creatively, respond empathetically to the needs of students, and remain resilient in the face of challenges. The following are some ways teachers can practice self-care to enhance their well-being. I encourage you to try them all:

- **Healthy Eating:** Plan and prepare balanced meals ahead of time, focusing on whole foods like fruits, vegetables, lean proteins, and whole grains. Bringing a healthy lunch and snacks to school helps you avoid unhealthy options and sustains your energy levels.
- **Positive Affirmations:** Begin each day with positive affirmations or reflections that set a positive tone for the day. For example, remind yourself of your strengths, express gratitude, or set a positive intention for the day.

  Examples of positive affirmations for teachers include:

  - *I honor the culture and experiences my students bring into the classroom, and I use hip-hop to make learning relevant and powerful.*
  - *I am a Master of Content, blending hip-hop's creativity with academic rigor to inspire and engage my students.*

- *Today, I will create a classroom environment that celebrates the voices, stories, and identities of all my students.*
- *I am a vessel of love, joy, and liberation, using hip-hop to uplift and empower my students every day.*
- *I am capable and prepared to make a positive impact today.*
- *I have the skills and knowledge to support my students' growth and learning.*

- **Develop and Maintain a Positive Teacher Circle:** Connect with fellow teachers who share values similar to yours and to share teacher experiences. Sharing experiences, advice, and encouragement with colleagues can help you feel less isolated and more supported.

As you end this book, I urge you to reflect on the power of your role as an educator. My journey from a young boy in the Soundview section of the Bronx to a passionate advocate for hip-hop pedagogy underscores the profound impact that culturally responsive teaching can have on students' lives. The classrooms where I felt seen, valued, and connected were the ones where my culture, my identity, and my love for hip-hop were acknowledged and celebrated. These moments of joy, love, and liberation weren't just incidental—they were essential.

Now, it's your turn to create these transformative experiences for your students. Start small, but start with intention. Integrate hip-hop not just as a tool for engagement but as a bridge to deeper understanding and connection with content. Whether it's through music, art, or the lived experiences of your students, use hip-hop to make your teaching relevant, inclusive, and powerful. Remember, the goal isn't just to teach content—it's to affirm identities, to empower voices, and to inspire a love of learning that transcends the classroom. By embracing hip-hop pedagogy, you have the opportunity to bring joy, love, and liberation into your classroom, creating a space where every student feels seen, heard, and valued.

Let this be your call to action— to use hip-hop as a means to not only educate but to elevate. Together, we can create educational environments that truly reflect and respect the diverse cultures, identities, and aspirations of all students.

AFTERWORD

CHRISTOPHER EMDIN

Dear Edmund,

I write this afterword at the beginning of winter. To write it as just a chapter set by the boundaries of pages in a book cannot capture the honor it is to write this. And so, it is equal parts afterword and letter. Read it as such and share it in the same way. Sometimes, it is important to let the world in on our conversations. It is the only way they can see themselves in us. It is also a powerful way to give permission to live vulnerably and honestly. In many ways, hip-hop is a collection of love letters. Each element writing to those who are moved by it. MCs write letters to the listener in each verse. Some verses are not metaphorical letters but actual ones. I'm thinking of when Nas wrote to his incarcerated brother on "One Love" or NLE Choppa, writing to his daughter. Even the body writes itself into the pages of the imagination when b-boys dance—suspending gravity and perceptions of the limitations of the body. . . . And so, I write this to you.

It's cold, the leaves have fallen from the trees, and the world feels stripped down to its essentials. The bright colors of autumn are gone, leaving a landscape of muted grays and browns. There's a quiet beauty in winter, a kind of pause that forces reflection. It is in the spirit of this season of reflection that I write this afterword. Juxtaposing it against the hopefulness of the foreword by my mentor and pedagogical guide, Gloria Ladson Billings. She wrote in spring to set the hope in this book in motion. I write of winter to offer my reflections after reading it.

Just as gardeners rest in winter, contemplating the growing season that has passed and planning for the one ahead, I find myself reflecting on what has been planted and nurtured in this work. That process has moved me to reflect on my own advocacy for hip-hop in education. It's been a tiresome and often lonely journey. When I started teaching, I had no reference point other than the eyes of the students who yearned for more than a scripted lesson plan. Reading this book has brought me back to those moments and offered me time to consider and reconsider so much about the seeds I have sown in my time as an educator and an educator of educators. In a world that dismisses and demeans hip-hop (especially when it is looking for a convenient scapegoat for its own deficiencies), the work to keep putting forth transgressive ideas often feels like perpetual winter. When you've planted the seeds but nothing seems to be growing, there is sometimes a temptation to scrap the gardening altogether. Each time a new effort comes that attempts to silence, erase, and ban what you know is essential to teaching, it feels like the soil is contaminated and the potential of spring is lost. I've had so many years of doubt—in myself, in this work, and lately, in this country.

When the last election passed, I asked, *Have the seeds planted in the field of education grown into something worth cultivating? Does the work put into planting those seeds have the power to be enduring? Do they need more care, more warmth, more light?* I have found answers to these questions in this book. Edmund, what you have offered in these pages are the care, the warmth, and the light to grow this work into something not just worth cultivating but formidable and enduring in its own right. This is not just a theoretical and practical framework for teaching and learning. This isn't even just a phenomenally strong argument for hip-hop in education but also a positioning of hip-hop as education. There is something radical about the assertions you are making here, and this book, through story, articulated experiences, descriptions, and frameworks, hits like a favorite verse being heard for the first time. This is Black Thought on Funkmaster Flex for me, beloved. Flow in the pocket. Steady. Heavy. Consistent. Bars! With the imaginative (re)introductions of the elements of hip-hop in each chapter, I feel growth for the field of education even in the frozen ground of winter. I am reminded that just because we can't see flowers blooming doesn't mean life has stopped. Beneath the frozen ground, roots deepen, storing energy for the burst of an eventual spring.

As the teacher who used hip-hop in his classroom that you described in the beautiful reflection early in the book, I'm humbled and deeply moved by the impact that our shared classroom experience has had on your life and practice as an educator and researcher. My goal has always been to make the sciences accessible, relevant, and joyful for my students. Your story is a testament to the importance of teaching not only the subject but also the student—meeting you where you are and honoring the cultural wealth you bring into the room, and in so doing, honoring my own. We, the teacher and the student, are at war with the same system that seeks to extract our humanity from us. As Mobb Deep says, "your beef is mine."

When I walked into that ninth-grade physics classroom as a teacher, I understood that my responsibility wasn't just to teach formulas or theories. It was to create a space where you could see yourself as capable, brilliant, and worthy of exploration in a field that so often overlooks the voices and identities of young people like us. Hip-hop was more than just a bridge to understanding—it was a way to affirm who you were. It was a way for us to connect science with the rhythms and realities of your world, making the content alive and meaningful.

Using 50 Cent's G-Unit chain as a pendulum wasn't just about explaining physics concepts; it was about showing you that science lives everywhere—in the music you love, the culture you embody, and the creativity you express. By anchoring lessons in something familiar and joyful, I hoped to spark curiosity, build confidence, and dismantle any barriers that told you the world of science wasn't yours to enter. But let me say this: your willingness to engage, your brilliance in drawing connections, and your growth are what made that classroom what it was. I taught with humanity because you and your crew all inspired me to be human. I held you to high standards because I saw the potential you carried. And as much as I gave in those moments, you gave me so much more in return—a reminder of why I teach and the confirmation that a radically different approach to education, rooted in hip-hop culture, had power.

As I read your book, I have come to understand that your knowledge on hip-hop in education is much more nuanced than mine. The moments where your unique genius leaps from the page are astounding and plentiful. You come with the experience of a participant in the culture, but also a student who experienced it in the classroom (something I never had). Then, as a teacher who taught with hip-hop and a researcher and scholar who grappled with both its hypocrisies and promise, you bring a vivacious vulnerability. That's not just alliteration. The youthfulness in your honesty and perspective is an incredible gift. What you have produced is a lifetime of experiences offered to the world with depth, sophistication, and practicality. It brings me immense joy to know that the many who will read this will be guided by your journey. My feeling now is that there is no need for hopelessness. The roots have strengthened in winter and across the world, in the classrooms of your readers, spring will come.

What you have created is more than the charge in the book title. It's more than just teaching like an MC. It is a step toward restitution for pedagogical violence committed against communities. This is "The Climb Back" by J. Cole. This is making a way for those whose ways of teaching and engaging with children were stripped away. As I tell my students when I see and hear the ways whitewashed versions of education history start shaping their thinking and teaching, Brown v. Board of Education meant that while students of color entered formerly White schools, the educational content, teaching practices, and institutional values remained rooted in the same biases that had upheld segregation in the first place. Black students were placed in an environment that dismissed their cultural identities, histories, and unique ways of knowing—perpetuating inequities even in the "improved" desegregated spaces. While the forces of "justice" integrated schools, they never integrated the curriculum or pedagogy.

As you allude to in the work, the failure to integrate the curriculum during school desegregation is directly tied to the rise and relevance of hip-hop as a cultural force. When schools desegregated but left curricula untouched, they ignored the cultural and lived experiences of Black and Brown students, creating environments where these students often felt unseen, undervalued, and disconnected. The classrooms I taught in, the classrooms you learned in, and the ones you taught in a decade later all inherit the same dynamic of cultural and emotional exclusion under the guise of betterment. Hip-hop emerged as a response to this exclusion—a way for marginalized youth to create their own spaces of feeling, expression, learning, and cultural affirmation. You and I are the product of exclusion, and now, through the labor in your text, the next generation does not have to suffer the same way. The book is bold, unabashed, and equipped with philosophy, framework, and experience. It is covered, as are you. Blessed, as are you. It is filled with promise and expectation that spring will come, and this time, we will teach the way we know and knew best; amplifying our ancestors' voices, and reclaiming stories of resistance, resilience, and creativity. Teaching like MCs.

—Christopher Emdin, Ph.D.
Maxine Greene Chair for
Distinguished Contributions to Education
Teachers College, Columbia University

REFERENCES

Adjapong, E. S. 2017. "Bridging Theory and Practice in the Urban Science Classroom: A Framework for Hip-Hop Pedagogy in STEM." *Critical Education* 8 (15).

Adjapong, E. S., and C. Emdin. 2015. "Rethinking Pedagogy in Urban Spaces: Implementing Hip-Hop Pedagogy in the Urban Science Classroom." *Journal of Urban Learning, Teaching, and Research* 11: 66–77.

Adjapong, E. S., and K. R. Kelly. 2023. "For White Folks Who Teach Hip-Hop—and the Rest of Ya'll, Too: Interrogating the Positionality of Hip-Hop Educators and Researchers." *Equity & Excellence in Education* 57 (1): 93–106. https://www.tandfonline.com/doi/abs/10.1080/10665684.2023.2200208.

Alexander, M. 2011. *The New Jim Crow: Mass Incarceration in the Age of Colorblindness.* New York: New Press.

Alim, H. S., D. Paris, and C. P. Wong. 2020. "Culturally Sustaining Pedagogies: A Critical Framework for Centering Communities." In *Handbook of the Cultural Foundations of Learning*, edited by N. S. Nasir, C. D. Lee, R. Pea, and M. Mckinney de Royston, 261–276. New York: Routledge.

Ambrose, S. A., M. W. Bridges, M. Dipietro, M. C. Lovett, and M. K. Norman. 2010. *How Learning Works: Seven Research-Based Principles for Smart Teaching*. San Francisco: John Wiley & Sons.

Anderson, R. E. 2023. "In the States: Addressing the Teacher Shortage." *Change: The Magazine of Higher Learning* 55 (4): 30–32.

Au, W. 2007. "High-Stakes Testing and Curricular Control: A Qualitative Metasynthesis." *Educational Researcher* 36 (5): 258–267.

Banks, A. 2000. "The Anatomy of the 1973 Party." Rock Bells. https://rockthebells.com/articles/dj-kool-herc-rec-room-party/

Baker, B. D., and M. Di Carlo. 2020. *The Coronavirus Pandemic and K–12 Education Funding*. Washington, DC: Albert Shanker Institute.

Baptist, E. E. 2016. *The Half Has Never Been Told: Slavery and the Making of American Capitalism*. New York: Basic Books.

Barton, A. C., and E. Tan. 2009. "Funds of Knowledge and Discourses and Hybrid Space." *Journal of Research in Science Teaching* 46 (1): 50–73.

Becht, A. I., K. Luyckx, S. A. Nelemans, L. Goossens, S. J. Branje, W. A. Vollebergh, and W. H. Meeus. 2019. "Linking Identity and Depressive Symptoms Across Adolescence: A Multisample Longitudinal Study Testing Within-Person Effects." *Developmental Psychology* 55 (8): 1733.

Blackmon, D. A. 2009. *Slavery by Another Name: The Re-Enslavement of Black Americans from the Civil War to World War II*. New York: Anchor.

Braniff, C. J. 2011. "The Effects of Movement in the Classroom." *Networks: An Online Journal for Teacher Research* 13 (1): 1–6.

Brown, R. N. 2013. *Hear Our Truths: The Creative Potential of Black Girlhood*. Champaign, IL: University of Illinois Press.

Brown v. Board of Education of Topeka, 347 U.S. 483 (1954). Justia Law. (n.d.). https://supreme.justia.com/cases/federal/us/347/483/

Burt, R. S. 2001. "Attachment, Decay, and Social Network." *Journal of Organizational Behavior: The International Journal of Industrial, Occupational and Organizational Psychology and Behavior* 22 (6): 619–643.

Burt, R. 2017. "Structural Holes Versus Network Closure as Social Capital." In *Social Capital: Theory and Research*, eds. N. Lin, K. Cook, and R. S. Burt, 31–56. New York: Routledge.

Caro, R. 1974. *The Power Broker: Robert Moses and the Fall of New York*. New York: Knopf.

Carter Andrews, D. J., and M. Gutwein. 2020. "Middle School Students' Experiences with Inequitable Discipline Practices in School: The Elusive Quest for Cultural Responsiveness." *Middle School Journal* 51 (1): 29–38.

Carter, S. 2017. "Jay-Z Pushes for Projects That Demand Social Justice: 'This Is Our Power.'" Guest column. *The Hollywood Reporter*, June 22. https://www.hollywoodreporter.com/news/general-news/jay-z-pushes-projects-demand-social-justice-is-power-guest-column-1014871/.

Chang, J. 2007. *Can't Stop Won't Stop: A History of the Hip-Hop Generation*. New York: St. Martin's Press.

Cherng, H. Y. S. 2017. "If They Think I Can: Teacher Bias and Youth of Color Expectations and Achievement." *Social Science Research* 66: 170–186.

Coleman, J. S. 1988. "Social Capital in the Creation of Human Capital." *American Journal of Sociology* 94: S95–S120.

Cook, L., and M. Friend. 1995. "Co-Teaching: Guidelines for Creating Effective Practices." *Focus on Exceptional Children* 28 (3).

Córdova, A., A. Caballero-García, F. Drobnic, E. Roche, and D. C. Noriega. 2023. "Influence of Stress and Emotions in the Learning Process: The Example of COVID-19 on University Students: A Narrative Review." *Healthcare* 11 (12): 1787.

Degruy, J. 2017. *Post-Traumatic Slave Syndrome: America's Legacy of Enduring Injury*. Portland, OR: Joy DeGruy Publications.

Dewey, J. 2005. *Art as Experience*. New York: TarcherPerigee.

Diemer, M., L. Rapa, A. Voight, and E. McWhirter. 2016. "Critical Consciousness: A Developmental Approach to Addressing Marginalization and Oppression." *Child Development Perspectives* 10: 216–221. https://doi.org/ 10.1111/cdep.12193.

Dossar, K. 1991. "Capoeira: An African-Based Tradition in the United States." *Journal of Physical Education, Recreation & Dance* 62 (2): 42–44.

Easley, D., and J. Kleinberg. 2010. *Networks, Crowds, and Markets: Reasoning About a Highly Connected World*, Vol. 1. Cambridge, UK: Cambridge University Press.

Emdin, C. 2010. *Urban Science Education for the Hip-Hop Generation*. Leiden, NL: Brill.

Emdin, C. 2016. *For White Folks Who Teach in the Hood . . . and the Rest of Y'all Too: Reality Pedagogy and Urban Education*. Boston: Beacon Press.

Emdin, C. 2023. Chris Emdin | SXSW Edu 2023 studio. March 8. YouTube. https://www.youtube.com/watch?v=rULeEJu6Hho.

Emdin, C., E. Adjapong, and I. Levy. 2016. "Hip-Hop Based Interventions as Pedagogy/Therapy in STEM: A Model from Urban Science Education." *Journal for Multicultural Education* 10 (3): 307–321.

Erikson, E. H. 1975. *Life History and the Historical Moment.* New York: W. W. Norton.

Eser, A. 2024. *Hip-Hop Industry Statistics: Dominance in U.S. Music Landscape*. Hip Hop Industry Statistics: Market Data Report 2024. https://worldmetrics.org/hip-hop-industry-statistics/.

Ferguson, R. F. 2003. "Teachers' Perceptions and Expectations and the Black–White Test Score Gap." *Urban Education* 38 (4): 460–507.

Fleming, N. D. 2001. *Teaching and Learning Styles: VARK Strategies*. Christchurch, NZ: Vark-Learn.

Foreman, J., Jr. 2018. *Locking Up Our Own: Crime and Punishment in Black America.* New York: Farrar Straus and Giroux.

Freedman, S. W., and D. Appleman. 2009. "'In It for the Long Haul'—How Teacher Education Can Contribute to Teacher Retention in High-Poverty, Urban Schools." *Journal of Teacher Education* 60 (3): 323–337.

Freire, P. 1970. *Pedagogy of the Oppressed*. New York: Continuum.

Gardner, H. 1993. *Multiple Intelligences: The Theory in Practice, A Reader*. New York: Basic Books.

Gay, G. 2002. "Preparing for Culturally Responsive Teaching." *Journal of Teacher Education* 53 (2): 106–116.

Gay, G. 2007. "The Rhetoric and Reality of NCLB." *Race Ethnicity and Education* 10 (3): 279–293.

Gay, G. 2018. *Culturally Responsive Teaching: Theory, Research, and Practice*. New York: Teachers College Press.

George, N. 2005. *Hip Hop America*. New York: Penguin Books.

Gogerly, L. 2011. *Capoeira: Fusing Dance and Martial Arts*. Minneapolis: Lerner Publications.

Golden, A. R., E. N. Srisarajivakul, A. J. Hasselle, R. A. Pfund, and J. Knox. 2023. "What Was a Gap Is Now a Chasm: Remote Schooling, the Digital Divide, and Educational Inequities Resulting from the COVID-19 Pandemic." *Current Opinion in Psychology*. https://doi.org/10.1016/j.copsyc.2023.101632.

Gonzalez, E. D. 2004. *The Bronx*. New York: Columbia University Press.

Gonzalez, M. F., and J. R. Aiello. 2019. "More Than Meets the Ear: Investigating How Music Affects Cognitive Task Performance." *Journal of Experimental Psychology: Applied* 25 (3): 431–444. January 28. http://dx.doi.org/10.1037/xap0000202.

González, N., L. Moll, and C. Amanti. 2005. *Funds of Knowledge: Theorizing Practices in Households, Communities, and Classrooms*. Mahwah, NJ: Lawrence Erlbaum Associates.

Gosa, T. L. 2015. "The Fifth Element: Knowledge." In *The Cambridge Companion to Hip-Hop,* edited by J. A. Williams, pp. 56–70. Cambridge, UK: Cambridge University Press.

Greene, M. 1978. *Landscapes of Learning*. New York: Teachers College Press.

Greenwald, A. G., D. E. McGhee, and J. L. Schwartz. 1998. "Measuring Individual Differences in Implicit Cognition: The Implicit Association Test." *Journal of Personality and Social Psychology* 74 (6): 1464.

Guisbond, L., M. Neill, and B. Schaeffer. 2013. "NCLB's Lost Decade for Educational Progress: What Can We Learn from This Policy Failure?" *Counterpoints* 451: 7–26.

Hamilton, L. S., B. M. Stecher, J. A. Marsh, J. S. McCombs, A. Robyn, J. L. Russell, et al. 2007. Standards-Based Accountability Under No Child Left Behind: Experiences of Teachers and Administrators in Three States. Santa Monica, CA: RAND.

Hammond, L. 2001. "Notes from California: An Anthropological Approach to Urban Science Education for Language Minority Families." *Journal of Research in Science Teaching* 38: 983–999.

Hammond, Z. 2014. *Culturally Responsive Teaching and the Brain: Promoting Authentic Engagement and Rigor Among Culturally and Linguistically Diverse Students*. Thousand Oaks, CA: Corwin Press.

Harro, B. 2000. "The Cycle of Liberation." *Readings for Diversity and Social Justice* 2: 52–58.

Heilig, J. V., H. Cole, and A. Aguilar. 2010. "From Dewey to No Child Left Behind: The Evolution and Devolution of Public Arts Education." *Arts Education Policy Review* 111 (4): 136–45.

Hoffman, B. G. 2017. "The Roles of the Griot in the Future of Mali: A Twenty-First-Century Institutionalization of a Thirteenth-Century Traditional Institution." *African Studies Review* 60 (1): 101–122.

Hötting, K., and B. Röder. 2013. "Beneficial Effects of Physical Exercise on Neuroplasticity and Cognition." *Neuroscience & Biobehavioral Reviews* 37 (9): 2243–2257.

Immordino-Yang, M. H., and A. Damasio. 2007. "We Feel, Therefore We Learn: The Relevance of Affective and Social Neuroscience to Education." *Mind, Brain, and Education* 1 (1): 3–10.

Jay-Z. 2011. *Decoded*. New York: One World.

John-Steiner, V., and H. Mahn. 1996. "Sociocultural Approaches to Learning and Development: A Vygotskian Framework." *Educational Psychologist* 31(3/4): 191–206.

Johnson, A. 2021. "Dirty South Feminism: The Girlies Got Somethin' to Say Too! Southern Hip-Hop Women, Fighting Respectability, Talking Mess, and Twerking Up the Dirty South." *Religions* 12 (11): 1030.

Johnson, Z. D., and S. LaBelle. 2017. "An Examination of Teacher Authenticity in the College Classroom." *Communication Education* 66 (4): 423–439.

Kendi, I. 2019. *How to Be an Antiracist*. New York: Bold Type Books.

Kozol, J. 1991. *Savage Inequities*. New York: Crown.

Krackhardt, D. 1992. "The Strength of Strong Ties: The Importance of *Philos* in Organizations." In *Networks and Organizations: Structure, Form, and Action*, edited by N. Nohria and R. G. Eccles, 216–239. Boston: Harvard Business School Press.

Krishnamurthy, S. 2023. *Fashion Killa: How Hip-Hop Revolutionized High Fashion*. New York: Gallery Books.

Ladson-Billings, G. 1994. "What We Can Learn from Multicultural Education Research." *Educational Leadership* 51 (8): 22–26.

Ladson-Billings, G. 1995. "Toward a Theory of Culturally Relevant Pedagogy." *American Educational Research Journal* 32 (3): 465–491. https://doi.org/10.3102/00028312032003465.

Ladson-Billings, G. 2013. "Lack of Achievement or Loss of Opportunity?" In *Closing the Opportunity Gap: What America Must Do to Give Every Child an Even Chance*, eds. P. L. Carter and K. G. Weilner, 11–22. Oxford, UK: Oxford University Press.

Lane, C. 2008. "The Distance Learning Technology Resource Guide." Retrieved May 5, 2011, https://www.tecweb.org/styles/gardner.html.

Lave, J., and E. Wenger. 1991. *Situated Learning: Legitimate Peripheral Participation*. Cambridge, UK: Cambridge University Press.

Lee, S., dir. 1989. *Do the Right Thing*. Film written and directed by Spike Lee. Distributed by Criterion, Universal Pictures.

Levitin, D. 2006. *This Is Your Brain on Music: The Science of a Human Obsession*. New York: Dutton.

Lin, N., K. Cook, and R. S. Burt, eds. 2017. *Social Capital: Theory and Research*. New York: Routledge.

Lindsey, T. B. 2013. "One Time for My Girls": African-American Girlhood, Empowerment, and Popular Visual Culture." *Journal of African American Studies* 17: 22–34.

Lippman, L., S. Burns, and E. McArthur. 1996. *Urban Schools: The Challenge of Location and Poverty*. NCES 96–184. Washington, DC: U. S. Department of Education, National Center for Education Statistics.

Lounsbury, J. W., B. C. Huffstetler, F. T. Leong, and L. W. Gibson. 2005. "Sense of Identity and Collegiate Academic Achievement." *Journal of College Student Development* 46 (5): 501–514.

Love, B. L. 2012. *Hip Hop's Li'l Sistas Speak: Negotiating Hip Hop Identities and Politics in the New South*. New York: Peter Lang.

Lynch, J. 2018. "For the First Time in History, Hip-Hop Has Surpassed Rock to Become the Most Popular Music Genre, according to Nielsen." *Business Insider*, 1. https://www.businessinsider.com/hip-hop-passes-rock-most-popular-music-genre-nielsen-2018-1.

Margolick, D. 2011. "Elizabeth Eckford and Hazel Bryan: The Story Behind the Photograph That Shamed America." *The Telegraph*, October 9. https://www.telegraph.co.uk/news/worldnews/northamerica/8813134/Elizabeth-Eckford-and-Hazel-Bryan-the-story-behind-the-photograph-that-shamed-America.html

Mascolo, M. F. 2009. "Beyond Student-Centered and Teacher-Centered Pedagogy: Teaching and Learning as Guided Participation." *Pedagogy and the Human Sciences* 1 (1): 3–27.
Maslow, A. 1965. *Self-Actualization and Beyond*. Center for Study of Liberal Education, University of Boston.
Mass Appeal. 2016. Cornbread lives. YouTube. October 26. https://www.youtube.com/watch?v=pXz_5TJbXr0
McKown, C., and R. S. Weinstein. 2008. "Teacher Expectations, Classroom Context, and the Achievement Gap." *Journal of School Psychology* 46 (3): 235–261.
McLeod, K. 1999. "Authenticity Within Hip-Hop and Other Cultures Threatened with Assimilation." *Journal of Communication* 49 (4): 134–150.
McNeil, L., and A. Valenzuela. 2001. "The Harmful Impact of the TAAS System of Testing in Texas: Beneath the Accountability Rhetoric." In *Raising Standards or Raising Barriers? Inequality and High-Stakes Testing in Public Education*, edited by M. Kornhaber and G. Orfield, pp.127–150. New York: Century Foundation.
Mensah, F. M. 2021. "Culturally Relevant and Culturally Responsive." *Science and Children* 58 (4): 10–13.
Milner, H. R., IV. 2007. "Race, Culture, and Researcher Positionality: Working Through Dangers Seen, Unseen, and Unforeseen." *Educational Researcher* 36 (7): 388–400.
Moje, E. B., K. M. Ciechanowski, K. Kramer, L. Ellis, R. Carrillo, and T. Collazo. 2004. "Working Toward Third Space in Content Area Literacy: An Examination of Everyday Funds of Knowledge and Discourse." *Reading Research Quarterly* 39 (1): 38–70.
Morris, T. D. 1996. *Southern Slavery and the Law, 1619–1860*. Chapel Hill, NC: The University of North Carolina Press.
Muhammad, G. 2023. *Unearthing Joy: A Guide to Culturally and Historically Responsive Teaching and Learning*. New York: Scholastic.
Murphy, R. J., S. A. Gray, S. R. Straja, and M.C. Bogert. 2004. "Student Learning Preferences and Teaching Implications." *Journal of Dental Education* 68 (8): 859–866.
National Center for Education Statistics (NCES). 2023. *Public High School Graduation Rates*. Condition of Education. U.S. Department of Education, Institute of Education Sciences. Retrieved May 24, 2023, from https://nces.ed.gov/programs/coe/indicator/coi/high-school-graduation-rates
National Center for Institutional Diversity. 2019. The Black Radical Tradition of Resistance. Medium. https://medium.com/national-center-for-institutional-diversity/the-black-radical-tradition-of-resistance-7277f09ef396
National Spiritual Assembly of the Baha'is. 1991. *The Vision of Race Unity: America's Most Challenging Issue*. Wilmette, IL: Baha'i Publishing Trust.
Necochea, J., and Z. Cline. 1996. "A Case Study Analysis of Within District School Funding Inequities." *Equity and Excellence in Education* 29 (2): 69–77.
Nestel, D., and T. Tierney. 2007. "Role-Play for Medical Students Learning About Communication: Guidelines for Maximizing Benefits." *BMC Medical Education* 7 (3): 1–9. https://doi.org/10.1186/1472-6920-7-3.

Nichols, E. J. 1976. Introduction to the Axiological Model. Paper presented to the World Psychiatric Association and the Nigerian Association of Psychiatrists. University of Ibadan, Nigeria.

O'Connor, C. 1997. "Dispositions Toward (Collective) Struggle and Educational Resilience in the Inner City: A Case Analysis of Six African American High School Students." *American Educational Research Journal* 34 (4): 593–629. https://doi.org/10.3102/00028312034004593

Pashler, H., M. McDaniel, D. Rohrer, and R. Bjork. 2008. "Learning Styles: Concepts and Evidence." *Psychological Science in the Public Interest* 9 (3): 105–119.

Peppler, K., and Y. Kafai. 2008. "New Literacies and the Learning Sciences: A Framework for Understanding Youths' Media Arts Practices." In *International Perspectives in the Learning Sciences: Cre8ing a Learning World*, edited by J. Moskaliuk, J. Kimmerle, U. Cress, G. Kanselaar, V. Jonker, P. A. Kirschner, and F. J. Prins, Volumes 2 (pp. 188–195). Proceedings of the Eighth International Conference for the Learning Sciences—ICLS 2008. Utrecht, The Netherlands: International Society of the Learning Sciences.

Ritter, S. M., and S. Ferguson. 2017. "Happy Creativity: Listening to Happy Music Facilitates Divergent Thinking." PloS ONE 12 (9): e0182210. .https://doi.org/10.1371/journal.pone.0182210

Rose, T. 1994. *Black Noise: Rap Music and Black Culture in Contemporary America*. Middleton, CT: Wesleyan University Press.

——. 2008. *The Hip Hop Wars: What We Talk About When We Talk About Hip Hop—and Why It Matters*. New York: Civitas Books.

Rosenthal, R. 2010. "Pygmalion Effect." In *The Corsini Encyclopedia of Psychology*, edited by I. B. Weiner and W. E. Craighead. https://doi.org/10.1002/9780470479216.corpsy0761.

Rosenthal, R., and L. Jacobson. 1968. "Pygmalion in the Classroom: Teacher Expectation and Pupils' Intellectual Development." *Urban Review* 3 (1): 16–20.

Rucinski, M. 2023. *Who Becomes a Teacher? Racial Diversity in the K–12 to Teacher Pipeline*. Rappaport Institute for Greater Boston Policy Brief.

Russell, C., and J. Shepherd. 2010. "Online Role-Play Environments for Higher Education." *British Journal of Educational Technology* 41 (6): 992–1002.

Sankey, M., D. Birch, and M. Gardiner. 2010. "Engaging Students Through Multimodal Learning Environments: The Journey Continues." In *Curriculum, Technology, and Transformation for an Unknown Future*, edited by C. H. Steel, M. J. Keppell, P. Gerbic, and S. Housego, 852–861.

Schwartz, S. J., S. A. Hardy, B. L. Zamboanga, A. Meca, A. S. Waterman, S. Picariello, . . . and L. F. Forthun. 2015. "Identity in Young Adulthood: Links with Mental Health and Risky Behavior." *Journal of Applied Developmental Psychology* 36: 39–52.

Sealey-Ruiz, Y. 2021. *Racial Literacy: A Policy Research Brief*. National Council of Teachers of English. https://ncte.org/ wp-content/uploads/2021/04/SquireOfficePolicyBrief_ RacialLiteracy_April2021.pdf.

Serpagli, L. P. 2017. "Social Media in the Science Classroom: Using Instagram with Young Women to Incorporate Visual Literacy and Youth Culture." PhD diss., Teachers College, Columbia University.

Serrano, S. 2015. *The Rap Yearbook: The Most Important Rap Song from Every Year Since 1979, Discussed, Debated, and Deconstructed*. New York: Abrams Image.

Stallion, M. T. 2020. "Megan Thee Stallion: Why I Speak Up for Black Women." New York Times, October 13. https://www.nytimes.com/2020/10/13/opinion/megan-thee-stallion-black-women.html.

Underwood, J. B., and F. M. Mensah. 2018. "An Investigation of Science Teacher Educators' Perceptions of Culturally Relevant Pedagogy." *Journal of Science Teacher Education* 29 (1): 46–64.

Universal Zulu Nation. n.d. Zulu Beliefs. https://www.zulunation.com/zulu-beliefs/.

Vygotsky, L., and M. Cole. 2018. "Lev Vygotsky: Learning and Social Constructivism." *Learning Theories for Early Years Practice* 66: 58.

Watts, R. J., M. A. Diemer, and A. M. Voight. 2011. "Critical Consciousness: Current Status and Future Directions." In *Youth Civic Development: Work at the Cutting Edge*, edited by C. Flanagan and B. Christens, Vol. 134, 43–57. Hoboken, NJ: John Wiley & Sons. https://doi.org/10. 1002/cd.310.

Watts, R. J., D. M. Griffith, and J. Abdul-Adil. 1999. "Sociopolitical Development as an Antidote for Oppression—Theory and Action." *American Journal of Community Psychology* 27 (2): 255–271.

Wilkerson, I. 2020. *The Warmth of Other Suns: The Epic Story of America's Great Migration*. New York: Penguin.

Willis, J. 2008. *How Your Child Learns Best*. Naperville, IL: Sourcebooks.

Yaribeygi, H., Y. Panahi, H. Sahraei, T. P. Johnston, and A. Sahebkar. 2017. "The Impact of Stress on Body Function: A Review." *EXCLI Journal* 16: 1057–1072.